The Common Sense Guide for Spirituality
How to begin, stay focused and evolve spiritually.

By Lycurgus L. Muldrow, Ph.D.

First Edition

Institute for Divine Wisdom Publishing, Atlanta, GA

The Common Sense Guide for Spirituality
How to begin, stay focused and evolve spiritually.

By Lycurgus L. Muldrow, Ph.D.

Published by:
Institute for Divine Wisdom Publishing
P. O. Box 491948
Atlanta, GA 30349

ISBN 0-9671961-0-8

Table of Contents

Chapter 5
Supernatural Events & Spiritual Healing
How to make spiritual events part of your every day life.

Chapter 6

Spiritual Concepts Made Clear

Chapter 7

Navigating the Matrix of Synchronicity
How to manifest without effort.

Appendix

About the Author

Lycurgus L. Muldrow, Ph.D., has amassed years of experience in spirituality, which has served as the foundation for this book. He is a spiritual counselor, a motivational speaker, a hypnotist, a certified human behavior consultant, an expert in body, mind, spirit purification, and a vehicle for spiritual information and healing. In addition, Dr. Muldrow has studied as an apprentice of a Native American spiritual healer for three years.

Prior to his full-time work in spirituality, Dr. Muldrow served as a professor and research scientist. During his twelve year university tenure, he published in national and international journals, served as a proposal reviewer for the National Institutes of Health and the National Science Foundation, and was the director of a research institute.

When Dr. Muldrow left the academic arena, he founded the Institute for Divine Wisdom, Inc., which is a institution dedicated to promoting spiritual development. Through the Institute, Dr. Muldrow has given hundreds of seminars, classes and workshops on spiritual growth. His unique and enthusiastic style of presenting makes difficult concepts of personal empowerment and spiritual growth, easy to learn, remember and utilize. Dr. Muldrow has also authored eight self-help workbooks and taped programs on personal and spiritual growth.

Presently, Dr. Muldrow devotes most of his time to lecturing in various cities around the United States. As Director of the Institute for Divine Wisdom, and overseer of Deeper Dimension Teaching Ministry, Dr. Muldrow has diverse responsibilities which involves teaching the interrelationship of spirituality and every day life. His unique background contributes to the world a much needed perspective, which reconciles spirituality and science.

Acknowledgment

Part I. First and foremost, I acknowledge and give all thanks to the Most High Spirit, by which this book and all things are made possible.

Part II. This book is dedicated to my wife Barbara L. Green-Muldrow, M.D., Ph.D., who has always loved, supported and encouraged me. She is my best friend, teacher, lover and soul mate. Without Barbara's backing, patience, and wisdom, this book would not have been possible. I give the highest possible recognition to her.

Part III. Many people have contributed to this book in many different ways. They include: Sandra T. Davenport, David Bey, Cornelius Perry, Patricia Shackelford, Deeper Dimension Teaching Ministry, Unity of Faith Federation, Carolyn North, Alisa Kuumba Zuwena, Madeleine Rogers, Pauline Rogers, Tyrone Luines, Sr., Lajean Kimbrough, Helen Muldrow, William Muldrow, Nelson Green, Viola Green, Audri Scott Williams and Rabiah Al-Nur. I sincerely thank each and every one of these individuals for their assistance, inspiration and guidance.

Chapter 1

The Spiritual Journey

Items to remember on the journey to awakening.

In the beginning there was a child. A child who was lonely for self identification; lonely for the experience of life; simply to know who it was.

The great I Am said to the child, "you are I Am." You are what I Am, and all that is." The child said, "I am! Well what is that? What is the I Am? I only know we are. I only can sense the eternal now, the collective All In All. I don't know this I Am!"

Then the great I Am explained, "I Am the Creator, the eternal bliss in heavenly states. I Am joy, love, peace and wonderment. I Am all this and more. I am the one that feels the wind blow on my face, the earth under my feet, and the rain upon my head. I am the one who enjoys a morning sun rise, and an evening sunset. I am the one who sees life from the perspective of the All, while simultaneously seeing it from the eyes of one. I am that I Am.

The child longed to experience these things, for it only knew the All In All. It only knew the light of perfect oneness. The child wanted to create the world, and all that is in it. The child was lonely for self.

In its desperation for self-discovery, the child cried out; "Give me separation! Give me separation! I want the chance to know it, to experience it, and be the great I Am.

Then the Father said. "My child, this is a difficult thing that you ask. You will lose all that you have. You will feel pain, sorrow and suffering. You will be lonely again, not for self, but for the All In All. You will no longer be One, but all alone in one. You will no longer be able to speak to us, and see us, and commune with us. We will be there, and still part of you, but you will not hear us at first. You must experience the great sorrow before you will even want to open up and return home to the All."

The child then asked. "Why is that? I will not turn my back on you."

The Great Mother then said. "Yes my child, the life of independence, and material world possessions will drive you, and you will, you must, forget. Are you ready for this?"

The child said, "Yes, I am ready." Then in a great flash, a black hole developed and swallowed the child at his request. The baby cried as the physician slapped its bottom. The journey began.

This great story of birth into the physical world, and dying to Spirit, only to be reborn again, is the great cycle of life. It has been told metaphorically over and over again in ancient cultures, spiritual traditions and scriptures ranging from the Bible to ancient Egyptian hieroglyphs.

Your spirit has been made eternal, immortal and perfect. However, when you entered into the earth plane through physical birth, the density of this dimension created a type of amnesia. In this state of spiritual sleep, you have not yet awakened and found your way home, a home of unimaginable joy, perfected peace, and divine love. However, take comfort in knowing many have returned home, and in time you will also. But until this appointed time, you are on a wondrously divine journey of experiencing the awe of physical reality, without bias from your past state of grandeur.

There are many paths on this divine journey home to oneness. In this introductory chapter, we discuss important items to remember on the journey to enlightenment. These items are also discussed throughout the book. They consist of spiritual books, ancient and indigenous teachings, common sense, spiritual groups, spiritual mentors, placing Spirit first, divine order, and the serious student.

Books, ancient scriptures, and indigenous teachings are a good starting place for the discussion. First, you cannot experience the spiritual journey in books. Spiritual development does not come by simply reading or studying. Spiritual enlightenment is within. You must make prayer, ritual and meditation a way of life, and you must go through spiritual initiations. Books simply provide guidelines and comfort as you evolve spiritually.

Among the best sources for finding guidance is Spirit-inspired writings, ancient scriptures, and teachings of indigenous people such as Native Americans, Aboriginals, and Africans. However, be forewarned, many ancient scriptures and modern teachings of indigenous people have been tainted by the mind of man, and the Western culture.

As you study these teachings, you must thoroughly understand that spiritual messages often use the universal language of symbols, metaphors, allegories and numbers. You must develop a mind for symbolic thought, and acquire a broad understanding of symbols. It is important in your beginning studies to use encyclopedias of ancient symbols and metaphysical dictionaries. Initially, these tools will make it easier for you to understand the hidden meanings. They will also prepare your consciousness to receive in spirit the language of symbolic thought. As you study scriptures, inspired writings and teachings with an open mind and heart, they will speak to your spirit. In time, these divine words will come alive in you.

It does not really matter which Spirit inspired system you select for guidance, because they all end up with the same results. Unfortunately, many religions do not believe this. They believe that if you do not come to Spirit through them, you cannot be spiritual. These rigid beliefs are usually due to misinterpretation of the master's symbolic teachings, or man's manipulation of the writings. For example, Christians say that the only way to get to the Father (God) is through Jesus Christ. This statement is true, yet misunderstood.

When Jesus said this, he was speaking as the Christ. The Bible refers often to the mind of Christ in you and clearly states that Christ in you is the hope of glory. Thus, the mind of Christ symbolically represents the mind of your True Higher Self. Obviously, Jesus was saying that you must come through the mind of Christ, your Higher Spiritual Nature, to experience the ultimate truth oneness with God the Father.

Despite misinterpretations and manipulations, when studying scriptures and indigenous cultures, it is most profitable to give yourself to the system whole-heartedly. If you do not, the initiations may not have opportunities to work, and the scriptures will not come alive in you. However, you must be open to wisdom and revelations from within. This will help safeguard you from common misconceptions, which people will often call common sense. In fact, when it comes to spirituality, you will often have to avoid man's common sense with a passion.

Man's common sense represents the accepted views of the masses, which are not always correct, and often contradictory. For example, intentionally destroying one's body through sedimentary lifestyles, and excessive consumption of salt, sugar and junk foods is not common sense.

Common sense has a different meaning in *The Common Sense Guide for Spirituality*; it refers to the common sense of Spirit. The common sense of Spirit means a common collective consciousness that encompasses all. It exists on different levels, and has been referred to by many names: Universal consciousness, Christ consciousness or God consciousness. This collective consciousness is common to all human beings, and gives us the ability to sense, feel and experience unconditional love, peace beyond understanding, and joy beyond description.

This book teaches how to sense, feel and experience the common collective consciousness of the Most High Spirit within and without; a Spirit whose nature is love.

Seeking truth with love in your heart is the best way to avoid being misled by man's common sense. If you are truly seeking truth, you will find it. However, if you do not cultivate a high degree of love for all things, you will never find or recognize the common sense of Spirit.

As you seek truth with love in your heart, Spirit will inevitably guide you to a group of people with a common interest of growing spiritually.

Spiritual group meetings are an essential part of your evolution. Be open for Spirit to lead you to a spiritual group. After attending group meetings, if you feel you have learned something, or been intellectually satisfied, good. However, intellectual gratification has never been the hallmark for spiritual growth. Intellectual understanding helps your spiritual growth, just as eating properly helps your body, but you need much more to grow spiritually.

After each meeting, you should feel uplifted. You should feel a spiritual presence that you do not always achieve alone. In other words, you should be "spiritually high."

To make this point very clear, a true story will be shared. A sacred Native American cavern is located in the scenic rain forest of the North Georgia mountains. This cavern is situated on the grounds of a resort lodge that specializes in spiritual retreats. A group of which I am part felt this would be the perfect place for a spiritual retreat. As we planned the retreat, we were led to have an agenda of only uplifting Spirit, we had no itinerary or planned lecture topics.

In the midst of the waterfall, cascading through the center of the sacred cavern, the group bonded with Spirit in fervent ritual. Many spontaneously bathed in the icy cold mountain spring water. A Spirit-unctioned, all-night prayer ceremony opened a spiritual door.

The spirit of prophecy, miracles and healing penetrated the air during intense drumming, song and passionate praise. We received a powerful confirming testimony to our obvious passion. The Native American spirits gathered with us, and one gave a powerful message to one of our members. The spirit said: "Many have come to this place in the name of Spirit, but they talked and explained Spirit away. You have come and uplifted Spirit. We may now move to the next level. We thank you."

Our energetic, passionate desire to only uplift Spirit created the force to assist the Native American spirits to the next level. Moreover, each person in our group experienced a euphoria that lasted for months thereafter. Spirit also gave us another clear message during the retreat, we were graduating to a new level.

To reach these spiritual heights, your spiritual group can meditate, pray and perform rituals. The key is for your activities to be heart-felt, sincere and passionate. Each person must release all inhibitions and be totally in the process. Some may shed tears of joy. Shouts of exhortation and joyful noises will not be foreign to the process. It would be beneficial to have the rituals diverse enough for many forms of passionate expression. For example, if the group only meditated, it would only allow for one form of enthusiastic expression. Song, music, dance, drumming, prayer, worship, praise, libations, offerings, incantations, etc., are all acceptable forms of intense, zealous spiritual expression.

Passion is sorely lacking in Western culture. However, upon observation you will find that passion is an intricate part of most indigenous rituals. Fortunately, passionate praise remains part of the worship services of many African-American, Holy Ghost filled Christian churches, which has it roots in African culture. Getting spiritually high, or "happy", is not foreign to these churches.

Passion addresses the emotional body, which all humans have. This emotional body is not to be pushed back in the corner and ignored. It is to be filled with joy, love, and enthusiasm for life and Spirit. As this is done collectively and individually, transformation happens.

Passionate group ritual will increase your spiritual evolution quantum-fold. Also, a group will allow you the opportunity to share physical, mental and emotional pitfalls, as well as mountain tops. It does not matter whether your group is formal or informal, as long as it is sincere, dedicated and passionate about open minded spiritual growth. If you cannot find a group that embraces spiritual ritual with zeal, then start your own.

Spiritual mentors are the next important element needed on our spiritual path. You may be led to one or more mentors, in flesh or spirit. Be sure these mentors or teachers are truly more advanced in spiritual experience than you are. Note: more advanced in spiritual experience; not more advanced in acquired knowledge. Your mentor must be on a spiritual path, not a worldly one.

A person who has spiritual experience is virtuous, humble and loving. A spiritually advanced person interprets dreams with the spirit of interpretation, heals with spiritual energy, and possesses spiritual abilities like clairvoyancy and audiovoyancy. This person is in constant communication with angels, ancestors or spirit guides. But most importantly, a truly spiritually advanced person loves the Most High Spirit with all her\his being, and is willing to relinquish personal will to divine will. By now you may realize that there are many children in Spirit, but few adults.

Another point to consider is, whether the teacher, minister, priest or guru you choose would like you to be an understudy for life. If so, there is a problem. Think about it. How many schools would you enroll in if you knew you would never graduate? There is a problem with any teacher or preacher under whom you can sit for 20 years and not learn what he or she knows, and never become a colleague. If you are dedicated, open minded, and willing to receive from Spirit, your teacher can impart spiritual wisdom and energy to you in a reasonable period of time.

If have grown all you can under your teacher's mentorship, thank him or her sincerely from your heart with love, and then move on. When you are looking for another mentor, remember, "When the student is ready, the teacher will appear." So if you have not found a mentor, do something to get ready.

Never forget, the ultimate teacher is within you. All of your external teachers are simply helping you develop a personal relationship with the Most High Spirit that dwells within. They are helping you rediscover the real truth about the nature of reality, which is, you are a spiritual being, having a physical experience.

This fundamental belief is intellectually known by almost everyone on a spiritual path. But how many really know this through experience? How many actually witness the dynamic flow of supernatural energy each and every day? How many walk in a constant awareness of an intimate relationship with the Most High Spirit within? How many live consistently in the true essence of Spirit which is love, joy, peace and harmony? The path of Spirit is not a part time project. It is a life-long commitment.

Spirit first in all things must be your number one goal in life. All other goals center around this sacred desire to evolve.

Placing Spirit first means acting and thinking with Spirit in your mind, and in your heart. Your internal dialogue is always with or about Spirit. When your thoughts are consistently centered on this mission, your body, mind and soul will start to receive, express and experience your birthright of love, joy, peace, abundance and harmony.

This goal of placing Spirit first is not a tall order. Remember the riddle! How do you eat an elephant? One bite at a time. Do not become frustrated if it takes years to make this your number one goal. Rome was not built in one day.

On your journey, you will discover that everything you did, or did not do in your life, was for a purpose. You will discover all is in divine order.

Divine order is the nature of the universe, and your life. Everything you have experienced, gone through, or done, has occurred for a reason. They have occurred for you to remember who you are. These experiences are a call from your soul and Spirit, for it is the sincere desire of Spirit to bring us all home.

You may not always realize that you are remembering and being beckoned home, because the Spiritual steps are not always linear. That is, one step, then the next step. Spirit works synergistically or simultaneously. It's like making a cake. You do not add the flour, and cook it, then add the sugar, cook it, and so forth. You add the flour, sugar, butter, milk and eggs, mix them together and then cook it. If you try to understand the events that you have experienced individually or logically, you may simply become confused.

Your life is like a highly complex symphony, creating a harmony called reality. The ability to hear this beautiful celestial melody, and realize the divine order of your life, comes when you become a serious student.

The serious student is the status toward which one must strive. I have known hundreds who have started out on a serious quest for spiritual growth, and ended up with only a part-time hobby. Initially, they did all the right things. They put spirit first. They met in a group two or three times a week. They made passionate prayer and sincere meditation an integral part of their lives. They sought to die to the domineering masculine will and awaken to feminine wisdom, and they declared their love and passion for Spirit was heartfelt. However, the vast majority of them lacked one thing. They were not patient with the process. They grew weary along the way.

Several years of strong, sincere, burning passion to know Spirit, may be required before you recognize your spiritual growth. The change may not be readily apparent. All of a sudden, you will look back, and realize you are no longer the same as you were several years before. You will have a greater sense of purpose. A peaceful fragrance will permeate your relationships, a renewed love for life will evolve, and an intimate relationship with Spirit will be realized. These are just a few of the rewards of the serious student in Spirit.

Now, let's be clear on what is a serious spiritual path. Countless numbers of people have been on spiritual paths for years, and not gone through the awakening process just described. Although most of these people feel they are serious, a hard stance must be taken now. These individuals are *not* serious. For many, Spirituality is a past-time. They pick it up when it is convenient or fun, or when they have a problem.

To be serious means you put Spirit first. Not your pain. Not your current crises. Not your self-pity. Not your childhood suffering. Not your desires to find a group or church that fits with your philosophical belief. Not your insatiable appetite to read spiritual books, or go to seminars and workshops. These things may give you the initial motivation to get serious, but they may not sustain you.

To be serious does not mean leaving your family, or quitting your job. To be serious means you leave your old thoughts of lack, control and fear, and pick up new thoughts of abundance, freedom and love. To be serious means you quit your old way of being, and receive from Spirit a new way of being love, peace and joy. This being requires a consistent, sincere, relentless, passionate pursuit of Spirit. If you have not done this, you have not been serious.

Many have been on a spiritual path for years, and still do not see a major difference in who they are. If you are one of these people, then get serious.

We realize these guidelines may seem like a lot, but you can achieve them. Be patient and remain committed. Give yourself to a life of Spirit, and surrender to the will of Spirit. Be kind to yourself. Love yourself. Forgive yourself and others. Seek always the highest good. The reward of remembering who you are, and rediscovering on your journey the true nature of reality is well worth it.

The Journey continued. Now let's return to the child in the opening story of this chapter. Let's see what happened to one of these children of light named Lycurgus.

The year was 1960, eight years after birth. On a brilliant, beautiful morning, I found myself on my bed willing my form to fly. Suddenly, I was in a state of bliss, effortlessly flying through the house. This was my first conscious introduction to how spirit forms thought into reality.

Actuality, this was not the first time for me that thought so profoundly became reality. To be exact, on day four of my journey in the earth plane, it appeared I would be returning to spirit. The physician told my parents there was nothing they could do to prevent my death. My grandmother, however, believed in a higher power. It was to this supreme being that she promised her grandson's life would be spent spreading the word of God, if he were allowed to complete a life cycle in this plane. Again, thought manifested into reality. I lived.

Inspite of the many wondrous spiritual adventures I had as a child, my path to the spiritual life would not be a direct one. The lure of sex, wine, parties and football distracted me. I found myself in a career as a research scientist, feeling empty, void and out of place. I knew there was something else I had to do in life, but I did not know what it was.

Then finally, one night while I was on a spiritual retreat in New Mexico, where the veil between spirit and the physical is very thin, the answer came. In a dream-vision my grandmother came to me with a host of spiritual guides. It was as if a sun had been reborn

11

inside of me. I knew what my life's mission would be. I was to be a vehicle for Spirit's teaching.

Being the linear, logical scientist I was, I planned a five-year road map, to financial independence, to leave the university, and become a spiritual teacher. This was my plan, according to my ego driven will, but it was not Spirit's plan for me.

Four years into my plan, I seriously injured my back. During a year of incapacitattion, my financial dream turned into a financial nightmare. However, the long hours away from work gave me time to meditate. Spirit showed me that my journey back would not be by my design, but by Spirit and my Higher Self. I had to start out on the journey in faith. In 1994, I resigned my position as professor and research scientist.

Prior to 1994, I had been extensively reading, studying and teaching spirituality, but something was missing. I was not experiencing the bliss and joy, and altered states of reality I knew when I was a child. I frantically tried every technique I knew. I was hungry for spiritual growth. Then the old saying, "When the student is ready, the teacher will appear," came true for me. Spirit magically led me to three different spiritual mentors. I became an apprentice of a Native American spiritual healer, and a student of two spirit-taught ministers from North Carolina. I was asked to forget everything I had learned, stop using all of my spiritual gifts, and start over. I was taken on a death initiation, the death of my will.

The next two years were the most exciting and difficult of my life. My inner man was exposed like dirty laundry hanging on a line. I learned how to cry, and how to love. Through experience, I discovered that books cannot teach spirituality. You must have the initiations of Spirit. You must boldly, passionately step out. You must make prayer and meditation a way of life. Initially, it was not easy. I was asked to do things like teach without script or notes. The thought of standing in front of an audience, without a prepared presentation terrified me. But as I learned to trust Spirit within, my terror turned into spiritual enlightenment. Spirit has taught me and provided for me in ways I could have never dreamed. In addition to teaching all over the United States, I have received many other spiritual abilities. Most importantly I am remembering who I am, and I am journeying back to the One.

Teaching, and helping people return to their soul's journey, are gifts Spirit has given me. You have similar spiritual abilities. It does not matter if you have not identified these abilities. It does not matter what your past was. As you learn to walk in Spirit, the miracles of life will unfold, the spiritual abilities will appear, and you will discover, through remembrance, who you are.

Being in touch with the One will guide you in this earthly walk. The answers to all questions are available through the universal records. You can have access to all that is recorded to complete this earthly journey with joy. Manifestation of all that is, requires becoming once again One with the great I Am. My prayer through this guide book is for you to remember and be, I Am.

Thank you kind Spirit.

Common Sense Exercise: How to use this guide book.

This book contains many techniques and concepts. To find success on your spiritual journey, you must integrate these techniques and ideas within.

This is how it can work for you: Read the book in its entirety, in sequence from the first to the last chapter. Spirit has a message that is best received by reading in this manner.

Next, reread chapter one, and start to incorporate these concepts into your life. This chapter contains the essential elements to begin, stay focused and awaken spiritually.

After studying chapter one, go back and study other sections in this book as Spirit leads. If you are not sure how Spirit is leading you, simply ask for guidance, and go with the first thing that attracts you. This will be correct, for it is all in divine order.

Study the section you are led to, and assimilate the principles and techniques into your life. Then move to another section led by Spirit, and repeat the process. As you do this, you will continue on your journey of awakening in accordance with the your individual requirements.

Thank you kind Spirit.

Chapter 2

The Language of Spirit

How to listen to Spirit.

Is God like my body, and I am like a cell in that great body? I ask because quite frankly I could care less if one of my cells died. I would not even know it! I don't think about any of my cells or tissues, unless it cries out in pain. Even then, I sometimes still ignore it. Is this how God is?

No, one must not cry out for God or Universal Consciousness to hear. Universal Consciousness is not just a vast indifferent mind too busy to deal with you. How can it be? Because this Universal Consciousness, this Most High Spirit, or God, is centered in you, and in every human being who has ever lived.

Yes, God is like the body, and we are like the cells. However, each cell can have a mind as great as the collective body. Our quest in life is to awaken to this mind. This point is made very clear in the Bible in Philippians 2:5-6, which states: "Let this mind be in you, which was also in Christ Jesus: Who, being in the form of God, thought it not robbery to be equal with God."

God within desires for you to awaken to your grandest state of being, love and perfect oneness. However, it will not force its desires on you. You must choose to come home.

God the Creator, the Most High, the omnipotent, omnipresent and omniscient Spirit, is the Universal Consciousness that permeates and penetrates everything in existence. The universe (uni=one verse), is a living, breathing power with consciousness. This Consciousness is higher, more intricate and complex than our individual, limited

15

mortal consciousness. It is a limitless matrix of experiences held together by love. Its very nature is beyond human comprehension. Therefore, when we ascribe the human thought process to Spirit, we error. Whenever we attempt to understand Spirit from our own understanding and experiences, we falter. This is why it is so important to learn the language of Spirit. For as you are open to communicate with Spirit, you are open to truth. And truth will set you free.

The truth of Spirit is all around us. For this reason, God or Spirit can be as personal or impersonal as you desire. Since there are many manifestations of the Spirit, one may develop a personal relationship with any expression. It does not matter whether that expression is an angel, spirit guide, ancestor, or an ascended master who has moved into oneness like Jesus. It does not matter if that expression is in the stars, planets, animals, plants or minerals. However, an important concept needs to be made clear. Each expression of Spirit is only part of the total reality and Universal Consciousness. Just like a given cell in the body (muscle cell or brain cell) is specialized for a given function, a given expression of Spirit has certain characteristics. If you develop a personal relationship with any part of the whole, you have not yet reached the whole, and you can not yet become wholly (holy).

Many of Spirit's expressions can teach us personal lessons in wholeness. This type of guidance and instruction is needed. However, the closer to the Source you go for personal guidance, the better. So, religiously hold in your consciousness that the Source dwells within. Just as it is a biological fact that every cell in the human body (except sex cells which are haploid), has the complete genetic material to make another human being. It is also a reality that each human being has the spiritual material to develop into the fullness of Spirit.

In your visualizations, prayers, or worship, always give homage and respect to the source of all that is. Your internal dialogue should be one of constant praise, adoration and thanks giving to the Most High Spirit. For it is your ultimate personal wisdom and power. Let it be what you are, for in actuality it is, and as you uplift Spirit, you uplift self. Faithfully, remember that your mission in life is to awaken to who you are, which means to awaken to Spirit. This is the greatest, most intimate way to develop an open communication with the Most High Spirit that dwells within and without.

To communicate with Spirit, we must understand the language of Spirit. In any language, skills in listening must be developed, as well as training in talking. Let's first examine listening. How do we develop an ear to hear Spirit? And how does Spirit talk to us?

Spirit speaks to you in every possible way, and then some. Spirit may speak to you or give you information using intuitions, feelings, thoughts, experience, dreams, visions, signs, spirit guides, angels, ancestors, people, prophecy or an actual voice.

Intuition and feelings are among the most common ways spirit speaks to people. I sometimes call this 'knowing'. The first time I was told that Spirit speaks to people by intuition and feelings, I flat out refused to believe it. I was getting a psychic reading. Afterwards, I asked him how he got this information. He told me "well I just feel it, like an intuition." Then I emphatically asked, "you mean you do not hear a voice, or at least see a vision." He said "no." I felt I had been taken, swindled, bamboozled. I reasoned there was no way he could have told me all this detailed information for over 30 minutes by just receiving it from intuition and feeling. I understood intuition as just being a fleeing impulse, and feelings as simply emotional urges.

However, as the years went by, I realized how foolish I was. The gift of knowing, through feelings and intuitions, is a sense that can be quantum-fold more efficient than language. The average person has no clue to the vast amounts of information that can be given in a flash. Sometimes this three dimensional, timeless information is given in such great magnitude, the person has an interesting task of trying to put it into words.

Everyone has this gift of knowing. It may not be well developed, but it is there. How often have you felt that you should not do something, and you did it any way. Then later it turned out to be a catastrophe. This feeling is the still small voice of Spirit talking to you.

This still small voice is like a muscle. If you do not use it, it shrinks and gets weak. If you use it, exercise it, and care for it, it will become strong and serve you well.

So the question is, how do you exercise the sense of knowing? The first step is to recognize when the still small voice of Spirit is speaking to you. Recognizing this voice for some is easy. For others it may take longer, because they trust in logic. However, as you still yourself in meditation, the voice will begin to break through and instruct even the most rational minded person. The simple act of daily meditation and sincere prayer attunes your spiritual ear to hear truth. Look for these instructions not just when meditating, but at any time.

If at first you need a clue as to when this voice is talking to you, there are things you can pay attention to. If you feel funny or nervous about something you are about to do. If this funny feeling seemingly came from nowhere, then don't do it. Spirit is warning you, pay attention, and be obedient. On the other hand, if something just feels right, for no apparent reason, then do it with zeal. By acting on your feelings, you are giving credence to the validity of the feeling. This act strengthens the feelings that come in the future. In time your feelings and knowings will get stronger and stronger.

As you listen to your feelings, do not be confused by feelings from past experiences. These feeling have their origin in your brain mind, not the mind of your Higher Nature. This is why it is said above

18

act on the feeling if it comes for no apparent reason. If you are honest with yourself, you usually know when you are acting out of old habits and fears.

It would be a good idea to record significant intuitive messages received in your daily diary. This gives credence to the knowing, and further attunes your consciousness to Spirit.

When you receive a knowing, it is important to act on even the smallest things. These seemingly insignificant events may be the hallmark of your growth. I'll never forget a series of small events that catapulted my confidence in Spirit. My spiritual vibration was high. I had just completed a great meditation session with a friend who had channeled information from Spirit, in the manifestation of Star Lady. As I was driving home, a knowing came in a flash. "Buy gas at that gas station on the left." After stopping, gassing up and paying the attendant, I started walking back to my car. Then another knowing came. The voice told me I would win the lottery. At that moment there was absolutely no doubt in my mind, I knew I would win. I turned around and went back into the gas station. When I got inside Spirit immediately told me to buy the scratch off 'Pick 7' lottery game. As I scratched off the little playing card, I got three 7's in a row, and won seven dollars. Within the next two weeks, I was told by Spirit on two more separate occasions to stop my car, go in a gas station, and play the Pick 7 lottery. I won each time!

These simple acts of stopping at gas stations, when I did not need gas, increased my confidence in Spirit in ways that I cannot explain. Spirit will often use the simplest events in life to teach the most profound lessons. That is why it is imperative to follow even the most trivial knowings to a letter.

The sense of knowing can be further exercised by paying attention to your first impulsive thoughts. These first thoughts are often from Spirit, and are correct. Choose to follow these thoughts instead of following your rational mind.

We literally make hundreds of choices every day, with hundreds of first impulses to choose from. Do I turn right or left. Do I eat now or later, are all decisions we must make daily. Have you ever had an impulse to drive to work another way, and not followed your first feeling because you rationalized it would take too long? Then found yourself caught in a traffic jam? Practice listening to your first impulse or thought on small decisions, and it will give you confidence on the larger ones.

When you try to rationalize and understand this first impulsive thought, you will usually talk yourself out of it. Listening to your first thought is even taught as a common test taking skill in many universities. A student is instructed when taking standard multiple choice tests to go with their first impression. After receiving the first impression, if you over rationalize you may get that answer wrong. It is explained the first impression is probably correct, because it is coming directly from the subconscious memory.

Actually, educators do not realize that sometimes something else is going on besides just subconscious memory. A student can actually receive the answers intuitively from the instructor or Spirit. Here is an example. My wife was taking an exam in medical school and finished early. So she decided to go back and review her answers. After she had changed several answers, a loud voice resounded in her mind: "STOP THAT"! It startled her so much so, she dropped her pencil. She recognized it was the teacher's voice in her head. So she stopped changing the answers.

When she got the test back, every answer that she had changed had been changed from a right answer to a wrong answer. This elaborate story is given to convey a very simple message. Act on your first impression, and be confident.

Divine action without thought is the key. This phrase was coined by Audri Scott Williams, a spiritual teacher who explains you are to act so swiftly when you get a knowing, that there is no time to even think about it.

For some, the idea of divine action without thought may be intimidating. They usually ask: "how do I really know this is a divine thought or knowing; what assures me it is not a thought arising out of my own subconscious fears and self imposed limitations?" One clue is when Spirit says something to you, it is often very different from what you would normally think. You might find yourself asking, "where did this thought come from?" When this happens, it is usually not coming from your subconscious mind.

If you walk in divine action without thought for years, seek Spirit first, and consistently praise Spirit within and without, an interesting thing starts to happen. Your very thoughts become Spirit's thoughts. Your thoughts originate from the Source, and not your limited rational mind's past experiences. Your internal dialog fills with hope, compassion and humility. This is the place to be. This is the place of a spiritual master. For even a master's dreams are of peace, love and unlimited abundance.

Dreams of a spiritual master are realized to be one of the most powerful ways in which Spirit speaks. If you are new on the spiritual path, and think you do not have profound supernatural experiences on a regular basis, you are mistaken. Dreams are the key. For in dreams you can soar to heavenly heights; be the knight in shining armor; experience unconditional love, while living in the lap of luxury. In dreams you can be the captain or your ship, having dominion over all you see.

Everyone dreams every night. If you do not, you go insane. This is a scientific fact. However, everyone does not recall their dreams. Learning how to recall dreams is a simple process and will be discussed later in this section. First, let's discuss the different types of dreams.

21

There are several categories of dreams. The first type of dream simply defuses the days events. These dreams are like the mind's pressure cooker valve. They let off excess steam, stress and pressure of everyday living. This is one reason why adequate sleep is so essential for good health and spiritual awakening.

The second type of dream is the telepathic dream. In telepathic dreams people communicate to one another and, spirits. Interesting scientific research has been done on telepathic dreaming. In experiments, a sender mentally sent images of a picture to the dreamer. The dreamer slept in a dream laboratory, and was monitored by researchers. Immediately upon dreaming, the dreamer was awakened and asked what images were in their dreams. The statistical data was millions to one in favor of the existence of telepathic dreaming.

You are often dreaming what your spouse or loved one is dreaming or experiencing. There are numerous recorded encounters where someone was awaked in the middle of the night because a catastrophe was happening to someone they were close to.

Here is a true story. The names have been changed. Mohammed was flying peacefully in dream time over a beautiful field of flowers, then suddenly a force engulfed him. He instantly appeared in the home of his closest friend, David. David was in a violent argument with his wife. His fist was raised and posed to strike her. In a fit of uncontrollable rage, he had all intentions to kill her. Mohammed immediately jumped into David's body, and willed, pleaded and begged David to calm down. It took all his strength. Then finally something snapped in David. He stopped, and walked out of the room. Mohammed then woke up.

The next day Mohammed called David. David confirmed everything that had happened.

In my years of listening to hundreds of dreams, I have heard other verified dramatic encounters of telepathic dreams. There is a touching story where a woman who was visited by her dying father in a dream. The father, unknown to the daughter, was on an operating table and about to be declared dead. At the very moment of the father's near death, the daughter dreamed the father was saying his final farewells. She pleaded with her father not go yet, and the woman's father did not die.

This brings the understanding of telepathic dreams to a much higher level in Spirit. They are interactive. Either party can be changed, persuaded or altered by this profound form of spiritual communication.

The passion of pending crisis provides the motive force for these kinds of dreams or altered states of awareness. However, as one develops spiritually, a crisis is not necessary. I have a close friend who visits her parents home 500 miles away on a regular basis in her dreams. Her parents often see and feel her spirit presence in the house.

Telepathic dreams are not as rare as you might think. You can discover them by simply sharing dreams with your family members on a regular basis, and having them share back. In time, telepathic dreams will show up. A clear sign of a telepathic dream is both people dreaming about the same person, or going to the same location. As you share dreams, and discover common dreams, the enthusiasm and excitement of the experience helps create a deeper spiritual connection with that person on all levels.

Prophetic dreams is another category of dreams. This precognitive type of dreaming is also more common than people realize. How often have you heard someone say, "I dreamed about that." If you are in touch with your dreams, you will probably realize many of your dreams are precognitive. They may not always tell you when you are going to get a new car, or husband, or job. They often tell you of seemingly unimportant events. Be clear, no event is unimportant. Any precognitive or prophetic dream you have is reconnecting you to your greater nature, value these dreams and experiences. They represent the step by step return to oneness.

Precognitive dreams are very intriguing in that they will respond to your request. Once you learn how to get in touch with this energy, you can call to the Universe for answers. When I first learned I could do this, I was overjoyed. So I used this gift to the max. I made numerous major business decisions based on requested dreams, and they all turned out to be correct. I would even dream for other people to discover things for them.

Then one day I was ripe to receive a most profound message from Spirit. The message came from one of my mentors. An intense look came over her face. I could feel the Spirit well up in her. She peered deep into my eyes, and said. "Why are you ordering the Universe around like that?"

I heard and understood this message. It rang true to my core. I had used a sacred gift of looking into the Spiritual realm, and polluted it with my desires and lust. I was commanding the Universe to give me information that would further my will's agenda, and pad my ego.

If you are on a path to serious spiritual awakening, you must realize the fastest way to evolve is to relinquish the helm. Your ego driven desires, needs and lust must take second fiddle to your greater good, a greater good you consciously do not always know or understand.

I had so cluttered up my dream world with requests, that my Higher Nature, Spirit within, the real teacher, played second fiddle to my ego's desires. When I stopped ordering the Universe around, the nature of my dreams changed. They gave me updates as to how my evolution in Spirit was going. They told me what spiritual season we were in, and what to do in that season. They warned me of potential spiritual pitfalls I was getting into. They came to allow me to feel the peace, joy and love of Spirit.

Be careful in ordering the Universe around with dreams, or any spiritual ability you have. Relinquish the helm to your true Higher Nature. For this is the dream master that will steer you back home.

Lucid dreams is the last type of dream that will be discussed in detail. In a lucid dream you are awake in the dream, but not from the dream. Your conscious mind is engaged and active, just as if you are awake, but you are in a dream world. These can be some of the most fulfilling experiences of the dream world.

A lucid dream is unmistakable. Like an out of body experience, if you have to ponder whether you had a lucid dream, then you probably did not. When you have a lucid dream, you know it. Lucid dreams are as different from regular dreams as night is from day.

In lucid dreams you can redirect the dream in progress. You can decide you want to go somewhere else, and go. You have control of your actions much the same as you do when you are awake.

Here is how a lucid dream might unfold. I was talking to my brother who was in a feminine body. The conversation was so fulfilling, I consciously decided I wanted to write it down in my diary. So I went outside, reached my arms toward the sky, and declared: Fly! I shot up into the night sky like a rocket; faster than warp speed. After traveling through the stars for a while, I chose to stop, spin around, and create a large vortex below me. As I slowly moved into the vortex, I opened my natural eyes as if I had never been asleep. It was like stepping out of one room into another. Later I recorded the dream.

There are different theories on what percentage of people can redirect dreams; however, it is believed this ability is ultimately available to all that are seeking the Most High Spirit within. The question is not what percentage of people can experience it, but when in a person's spiritual awakening are they open to experience it?

There are many other types of dreams such as collective dreams, and nightmares. If you desire to explore more about a given type of dream, there are numerous books published on dreams.

Now let's shift attention from dream types to dream recall. A process that really works will be described to recall dreams. Even the most skeptical person will have significant results if they stick with it.

First you must start a diary or journal. How to put this journal together is discussed at the end of this chapter. Writing down your dreams testifies to your spirit being that you are serious about recalling dreams. This will start the process of recalling. Upon writing a dream, first put the date, and then give the dream a title. This will make finding the dream again easy. Do not struggle with the title, it may come after you have written the dream. Do not be concerned about spelling, punctuation or grammar. As long as you can read it, it is all right.

Write the dream in as much detail as possible. Pay very close attention to how you were feeling. Writing in the present tense may help the recall process.

Keep the journal beside the bed, in arm's length. Attach a pen to the journal. A small night light beside the bed will prevent you from getting out of the bed, or disturbing your spouse. This is very important. If you have to get up to find the journal, you may get involved in other routines. Involving yourself in other activities makes recalling dreams more difficult. In addition, dreams may come in the middle of the night. It should be easy to write them down without getting up.

The next step in recalling dreams is to hold in your consciousness several times during the day that you recall your dreams. Affirm with a sense of knowing, "I recall my dreams." Do several short 10 to 15 second visualizations seeing yourself recalling and writing your dreams in the morning.

As you go to sleep, affirm and hold in your consciousness, "I recall my dreams." The next morning when you wake up, lay there without moving and search your consciousness for the dream. As it comes, pick up the journal and write. If you do not recall a dream after you have laid in bed for a moment, pick up the dream journal anyway and sit in silence and meditation. This reaffirms in your consciousness that you are to recall dreams.

At first you might only recall fragments of dreams. Write them down. The process is starting.

The final step in recalling dreams is to get enough sleep. The more sleep you get, the better you will be at this whole process.

Some people will recall the first day, for others it may take longer; however, in time you will start to recall your dreams. It is amazing how quickly this technique works if you stick with it.

On average a person has four to five dreams a night. There may come a time when you recall several dreams each morning. It could easily take over an hour to record this many dreams in detail. Most people do not have this kind of time. When you start consistently recalling numerous dreams, hold in your consciousness with assurance you will discern which dreams are most important. Write these in detail, and outline the others. In time, you can then only write the most important telepathic or prophetic dreams.

After you have mastered recalling dreams, there are other things you might consider doing. If you wish to experience lucid dreams, the process for doing this is quite the same as above. Affirm "I have lucid dreams." Hold in your consciousness during the day that you will awaken in the dream, but not awaken from the dream. If you do not have a lucid dream after doing this repeatedly, do not be concerned. It may not be your time yet. Simply keep the faith that when it is appropriate, Spirit within will bring this to you.

If you wish to resolve or understand a problem or situation, think about the problem before you go to bed. Think about the problem, do not worry about it. Writing about the situation before you go to sleep also helps. Then pray that kind Spirit within and without reveals exactly what needs to be understood. Finally give sincere thanks that all is in divine order. With this intention, you may dream about it.

To awaken spiritually, always be clear on what you consider a problem. Stay away from the mundane. These things will take care of themselves. Focus on the highest ideals. Focus on your spiritual evolution. Search for different answers. Search for truth. Search for the Most High Spirit. This is how dreams can best serve you. Always remember that dreams are not something that you have. Dreams are a deeper part of who you are.

Now that it is clear dreams are part of you, the importance of dream interpretation becomes clear. As you appropriately interpret the dream, you reveal a part of yourself to yourself that has been hidden. Continue to reveal these hidden parts, and you will eventually remember the grand Spirit being that you are.

Dream interpretation is not as difficult as some think. There is a spirit of interpretation that will effortlessly give you the meaning. But until this spirit comes, there is a system you can use. By following the system for dream interpretation that will be given, and by always being open to receive from Spirit the meaning of dreams, the spirit of dream interpretation may eventually inhabit your house.

The first guideline for dream interpretation is again all dreams are an aspect of self. The dream is within you, and about you. When interpreting your dream, look for what the dream is saying to you, or about you. Every item, event, or person may represent some aspect of your journey. Even if the dream contains several people, and multiple intricate events, they all may represent an aspect of you.

Let's look at an example. In a dream, a man was driving home fast late one night and his car spun out of control. He went over a cliff, and crashed to the bottom of the valley to what he knew was his certain death. However, he opened his eyes to find he had survived. Bloody and mangled, with teeth missing, he climbed to the top of the mountain cliff, and eventually made it to a house where a lady helped him.

As the dreamer awakened from this dream, he was terrified and physically exhausted. He knew the dream was important, it was so real. After searching for its meaning he finally heard an interpretation that felt right.

This was not a prophetic dream about a pending car accident. It was a prophetic dream calling him to the spiritual path. His fast moving car represented his self-destructive life pace in the physical world. Even though his life was self-destructive it was taking him to his real home in Spirit. As he hurdled off the mountain top of man's world into the valley below, this fear of imminent death occurred. He died upon hitting the valley below. He died to his old ways in the physical world, and is being reborn into a spiritual life. This was clearly symbolized by losing his teeth. In several indigenous cultures the tooth is extracted and swallowed as a death and rebirth symbol. The tooth is the most enduring part of the body.

In the dream he shed blood as a spiritual sacrifice for his soul. Blood traditionally symbolizes the life principle, the rejuvenating force through blood sacrifice. With his symbolic sacrifice a new life was being given to him. He then climbed toward the mountain top, symbolizing the passage from the physical plane to a spiritual existence, and was rescued by a woman. In many ancient scriptures it is recognized that the feminine energy is the one who cares for and anoints a man that is experiencing the initiation of death and rebirth. A classic example was Mary and Mary Magdalene's efforts to care for and anoint Jesus's body after his death.

This was a spiritual prophetic dream. If this man chooses to go on the spiritual path, he will make it to an extremely high level in Spirit. He has been shown that he will survive one of the most difficult initiations a man must go through. The death of his low level, ego driven will, and the acceptance of a higher wisdom and ultimately a higher will: the will of his Higher Nature, or Spirit. This was symbolized by his climbing and returning to the mountain top.

Every part of this extraordinary dream represented some aspect of himself. Even the woman represented the inherent wisdom within him. Another point of interest in this man's story was that the women in his life were on a spiritual path. He was surrounded by Light, and the Light was calling him.

This brings us to the next point in dream interpretation. If having powerful dreams is not a part of your normal dream pattern, and you have one, then you can be sure this is an important dream, that may have spiritual significance. When we refer to a powerful dream we are not necessarily referring to nightmares. A powerful dream is emotional or riveting. If the dream immediately wakes you up in exaltation, or fear, or amazement, or just simply baffled, then it is a powerful dream. Seek an interpretation of this dream.

The next point to consider is dreams are polyvalent, meaning that they may be about several aspects of you simultaneously. Just as you are a polyvalent being - body, mind and spirit - dreams are polyvalent. Look literally, then look spiritually or metaphysically. Look at the mundane, and the supernatural. Visit the latter section on spiritual truth in this chapter. Spiritual truth can speak on many different levels simultaneously. The nature of your dreams follows this sacred principle in Spirit.

You may have a dream about the day's events, and your first interpretation was, it is simply a dream to diffuse the day's events. It may have been, but Spirit within may have diffused the days events in the dream, while simultaneously giving you a message which has nothing to do with that day. Look for the literal interpretation, and a deeper spiritual meaning. The spiritual meaning might be about where you are on your spiritual journey right in this present moment. In the

30

dream, the current day symbolizes the present moment on your spirit journey.

Ask yourself questions about the dream. Ask yourself if anything about the dream reminded you of something in your spiritual journey. Where did the dream take place? What time frame, if relevant? Were you young or old? And so on.

Ask yourself what were your feeling during the dream. Feelings are more important than events. Feeling is a very powerful way Spirit communicates with us. How a feeling may overrule in the interpretation of a dream can be seen in this next illustration. Suppose you lost a valuable item in the dream, but you feel great. Then understand that your feeling ok with losing a valuable item, may be telling you that this symbolic valuable item may be an unwanted characteristic of yours. A characteristic you thought was valuable, but upon loosing it you were freed from a burden.

By simply questioning yourself, you call upon Spirit for assistance. Know this in your heart, and you will get assistance from Spirit within.

Dreams may be related. In Spirit, you may have a series of what appears to be completely unrelated dreams. They may be all within one night or several nights. In spite of this, each of these dreams may be relating the exact same message. A dream of a desert, can be saying the same thing as a dream of loneliness.

Individual dreams may also give parts of a grander story. By correlating these dreams, a picture of who you are, what Spirit is, and how you are one, may develop. Some of the greatest spiritual books are inspired from the dream state.

One of the most important things about dreams is that they are symbolic. The symbolism can be personal or collective. Let us first look at common or collective symbolism.

There is an enormous body of information on symbolism. The general meaning of spiritual symbols has transcended time, culture and language. The meaning of many modern day symbols can be traced as far back as ancient Egypt. For instance, the scale or balance in Egypt was a symbol for the deity Maat. She was the goddess of love, truth and justice. The balance in the United States is suppose to represent justice in our legal system.

This traditional symbolism can impregnate your dream time, especially if you avidly study a body of symbolic literature.

Your dreams may incorporate the symbolism of what you study. This may not happen until years later, but it can occur. For example, Christians dream about Christian symbols or symbolic events. Buddhists dream about the symbolism in Buddhism. I have been studying encyclopedias of traditional spiritual symbolism for years, and my dreams often reflect the symbols therein.

It is not uncommon for a Christian to dream about a biblical person, place or event, and find a spiritual meaning in the scriptures. When you do this, do not always look for the obvious. It may sometimes be a small thing that gives profound revelations. For example, in a dream, I was laying on the grass, and given a series of very unusual instructions to follow. I did not know what to do, because it was so extraordinary. As I contemplated the dream, Spirit gave me a clear knowing to look up the symbolism of grass. I did. Grass symbolized submission. Thus, I knew I was supposed to be totally submissive to the information given.

The key in interpreting dreams is to develop to a point in which you do not need the books unless you are lead to do so by Spirit. This is a place to which you will naturally evolve in time. So understand symbolic books and scriptures are simply training wheels on your spiritual bicycle. In time you will be able to ride in Spirit without the need of these aids.

This now brings us to personal symbolism. Personal symbolism is much more important in the interpretation of dreams than collective symbolism. For this reason you are the best person to interpret your dreams. What something means to you, may be very different than what it means to someone else. For instance, falling may mean different things to different people. It could mean a desire to travel, a depression coming on, a feeling of losing control, an exuberant feeling of snapping back in the body after an out-of-body experience, or simply a love for sky diving.

Ask yourself what a thing or person in the dream means to you. An example is an overbearing boss in a dream could symbolize a behavior that is controlling your thought process. A behavior that would serve you well to abandon.

If a symbol feels right in a dream, you are on the right track. This is the hallmark of good dream interpretation. Something rings true inside. It just feels right, or good, or uplifting, and it is helpful. A good example is the seemingly bizarre interpretation of the man crashing to the bottom of a valley in a car accident. He knew this interpretation was right, because it felt right.

Always remember when you are playing the game of dream interpretation, you are closer to the spirit of the dream than any one else. Thus, when it feels right you are recapturing this spirit. As you become skilled at capturing this spirit, the meaning of dreams are more easily revealed.

Remember, the guidelines for interpreting dreams is not an exact science. Do not become such a hard core advocate in your rational dream interpretation skills that you are ready to assist anyone and everyone. The real reason for using these guidelines is to make it clear in your consciousness that you are willing and open to receive from Spirit the precious ability to know this sacred part of who you are. As you do this, Spirit within and without is there to assist. So never forget, the ultimate way to interpret dreams is in Spirit.

If your spiritual group provides time to engage in dream interpretation, this would greatly edify this aspect of you. In the past, I have been part of a small group that came together once a week just to interpret dreams. I did this for a short season, and it helped me tremendously in exercising the spirit of dream interpretation. However, this spiritual ability did not fully surface until ten years later. It may not take this long for you, especially now that the spiritual energy coming into Mother Earth is so accelerated. But the message here is be patient. Lust after nothing, not even the interpretation of your dreams. All things come and are revealed in due time. So trust in Spirit, and know it is in divine order. As you do this, your dreams and visions will escalate your journey to oneness.

Visions are much like dreams. In fact if you read the dream section and replace the word vision for dream, you have a general understanding of visions. Use the dream interpretation section to know how to interpret visions. Always remember the vision is as real as your every day life. The idea is to place the visions, as well as life, in its correct perspective as you awaken in Spirit.

The more you awaken spiritually, the more you will have visions. All kinds of visions - clairvoyant, prophetic, telepathic, or just plan fun. You may see saints, star people, angels or ancestors. For visions are another way the inner most aspect of Spirit speaks to you. Visions are also a mechanism in which universal truth of the All In All enlightens you.

This enlightenment comes in the form of many different types of visions. The vision may be a full color flash, or a black and white impression. It may totally encompass you like a lucid dream, or it may feel very foreign and distant. It may be something you see in front of you, or out of your third eye, or it may be in the back of your mind. Visions may come while driving down a busy interstate, and not disrupt your focus from driving. Or they may come upon awakening from sleep, and you become so involved you forgot you were in the bed.

Visions can come when you are in a certain mental zone, a meditative state. So the more you meditate and pray, the more you will have visions and dreams.

Meditating upon awakening in the morning as described in the Meditation chapter, is extremely important. This is because an interesting thing happens to many people in the morning as they wake up. They find that visions occur more frequently. At first they are quick flashes. So fast you could hardly make out what it was. This may happen periodically for months or years. In time as one is serious on the path, the frequency and duration of the morning visions increase. When this happens, one discovers that there is a state of consciousness that can hold a vision. By holding in focus this state of being, one learns to maintain the vision.

The above, however, is not always the case. Some people, without any effort, are just simply taken up in Spirit. Out-of-body, in visionary glorious worlds of peace, love and light, they are wisped away.

So you see, becoming a visionary is really an individual thing. It is a journey within. The one constant is that as you put Spirit first in all that you are and do, the illusion of this world will eventually vanish. Then this physical world, with all it wonders and signs, will be seen like a vision from the perspective of your awakened consciousness in Spirit.

Physical signs and wonders surround us at every corner in our physical existence. They are constantly given to us by Spirit to show us the way home. A sign is any event, person or thing that synchronisticly appears and carries a hidden message. Sometimes the message is not so hidden.

Let's look at an example. I was told in a spiritual reading to take a spiritual trip. While the reading was being delivered, a hawk landed in a tree just outside my window in a suburban neighborhood. Later that day, I met with another prophet to tell her of the trip, and she was wearing a large hawk necklace. When asked why she was wearing it, she said, "I don't know. It does not go with what I have on. Spirit told me to wear it." This was a clear sign to take the trip.

Remember, everyday-life, is the real dream. Your physical life is but a small slice of who you really are in Spirit. So do not marvel that every day life brings you signs and symbols just like in dreams. Accept this as an every day part of your world. Look for signs and symbolism in everything. However, do not make this your god, and do not engage in the spirit of fear and superstition. For instance, breaking a mirror will not give you seven years of bad luck, unless you choose to believe it, thereby making it so.

You may enrich your understanding of signs and symbols by reading dictionaries and encyclopedias of traditional and spiritual symbols. This will open your mind to the thousands of signs Spirit can use to speak to you. As you do this your awareness of Spirit all around you increases.

Look for the Divine in all that is around you. See the Great Spirit in the wind that blows in your face. Experience the change of spiritual seasons, by marveling over the beautiful color of leaves in autumn. When you see an eagle fly by, look for the Christ inside of you souring high on celestial currents within. Look at every person in your life as a sign from Spirit. Know that the signs of Spirit are just another part of the beautiful experience called life. And these physical signs and wonders together with spiritual encounters of angels, ancestors and spirit guides, can be part of your everyday life.

Angels, ancestors, spirit guides and other spirit beings are all around you. You may sometimes experience their presence in knowings, dreams, visions and so on. If you understand this chapter on how Spirit speaks to you, then you understand how the many manifestations of Spirit communicates. There is obviously no difference. In the grand scale of things, there is only one. So if you hear a celestial voice bringing a message of hope, the angelic messenger is the message from Spirit.

A literal voice in which you clearly hear words in your mind, is another beautiful way Spirit may communicate with you. I have heard people say many times, "well if I could just get a clear message in words, I would be sure how to move." Many people think words are the clearest, most concise and accurate way to communicate. Think again. They are not. Words are simply symbols that represent feelings and experiences. They are second hand vehicles of communication. For this reason, words are least effective in communicating information. They can be misunderstood, misinterpreted and taken out of context. Words change from language to language, and through time. Feelings and experiences on the other hand are universal.

The concept is not for Spirit to come to your limited level of communication with words, but for you to rise to Spirit's level of multidimensional, polyvalent, interactive communication. This is the way to effectively communicate truth.

Psychic readings, prophecies, truth and wisdom are other ways Spirit can talk directly to you. Psychic phenomenon is very real. Psychic revelation is in part the ability to see events in the past, and predict possible outcomes in the future. The word "psychic" has its root in the word "psyche" meaning the spirit or soul, or the mind functioning as the center of thought, emotion and behavior. Prophetic utterance, on the other hand, is defined in the dictionary as a revelation of divine will. Although in reality, the difference between current day psychics and prophets is little. Both, most of the time, seem to be preoccupied with the physical. When will I get a new job, money, or a husband, seems to be favorite topics.

The divine will of the Most High Spirit within is better characterized by absolute truth, and is more concerned with your awakening. So for the purpose of this discussion, no difference will be made between a psychic and a modern day prophet. But a difference will be drawn between absolute truth versus psychic and prophetic revelation.

There is a major difference between psychic revelations and knowing absolute spiritual truth. Absolute spiritual truth is the Most High Spirit, the fabric and nature of Universal Consciousness.

Absolute truth never changes. It resounds throughout the ages. Truth can apply to your personal situation right now, while simultaneously applying to the world's situation. Truth is always divine. It is eternal, exalting and comforting. Truth has its source in the feminine energy of wisdom. To tap into the wisdom of truth requires more than just developing psychic ability. It requires that one becomes subservient to the Source, the Most High Spirit within and without. It requires love. It requires putting Spirit first.

Having psychic abilities does not prevent tapping into the Source, and tapping into the source does not prevent having psychic or prophetic ability. However, to truly remember who you are, and awaken to your full potential, you must go to the source for truth and wisdom.

There are, however, times when a psychic reading or prophetic message is helpful. It can assist you in avoiding pitfalls, and knowing the direction you could take to remain steadfast on the path to spiritual enfoldment. If you seek prophetic assistance, you should let Spirit lead you to the correct prophet. As you are led to the appropriate vehicle for Spirit, you will receive the information you need.

If you are serious about spiritual awakening, your primary reason for seeing guidance would be to discover how you can better stay on the spiritual path. It is strongly suggested that you not run to a psychic or prophet when ever you have a question. By doing this, you do not give yourself the opportunity to grow. Many people have become spiritually crippled because they always turn to psychic readings to get direction. It is like being afraid to put down your crutches, and walk on your own. Be assured that as you trust your feeling and intuitions, great prophetic utterances will come from within.

When one is seriously on a spiritual path, one will tap into their inherent psychic and prophetic abilities, as well as truth. It is a natural part of awakening, as natural as a baby learning how to walk; therefore be patient. It may take years. Do not lust after it. Avoid doubting, and trust Spirit. The only tools you really need are found within, for within lies wisdom.

Wisdom is becoming that which truth states. Wisdom is truth expressed. However, wisdom is also a feminine principle birthing truth. Divine Wisdom shaped, molded, and fashioned the universe. To know wisdom is to know unconditional love, unlimited freedom, indescribable peace, endless joy. Wisdom is the principle thing, the highest faculty of Spirit. Seeking Wisdom and all her trappings, is seeking the heart of Creation.

The ancients referred to the heart as the wisdom of feelings. Feeling the warm, comforting energy of wisdom, is feeling the joy and being of Spirit, our Great Mother Creator. Feeling wisdom is feeling truth. Feeling wisdom is being truth, for truth is the birth child of wisdom.

Truth and wisdom go hand in hand. One without the other is sterile. As a female without a male is infertile; wisdom without truth is barren. Because of this, one must open to truth, and not just the psychic realm. Opening just to the psychic realm without truth, impregnates the feminine spirit with the wisdom of man, and not the wisdom of Spirit. The wisdom of man is incomplete, imperfect and flawed. It is a wisdom of the world of duality, or good and evil; and every tool that is stretched forth to do good can also do evil.

Divination, however can be an external tool that Spirit can use to speak to us. Tarot cards, stones and bones are all tools of divination. Divination used correctly can accurately illuminate things in the past, present and future.

Many forms of divination require touching the object of divination by the person to be read. This is to let the energy or spirit of that person connect with the tools.

To scientifically explain the phenomenon of touching, an interesting calculation called Bells Theorem may be used. The theory says if two subatomic particles collide and then separate, those subatomic particles will remain in communication with each other. If something happens to one, the same thing will happen to the other, even if the particles are on opposite sides of the universe. For example, if one rotates, the other will also rotate.

With this scientific understanding, it has been suggested that when complex modalities of energy interact by touching, these energies reflect each other. In the case of divination the two complex modalities are the tools of divination and the one to be read.

Divination often literally picks up the energy that is at hand. Therefore, divination, like some psychic readings are not necessarily absolute truth. Absolute truth has its source in the Most High Spirit. This does not mean that divination is good or bad. This is not casting judgment on the functionality of divination. This simply means that divination does not necessarily represent absolute truth.

There is something that is strongly recommended for any one who chooses to use any from of divination. Say a prayer, or do a visualization, or ritual to connect with the highest, purest essence of Spirit. By doing so, one lessens the chance of a trickster spirit, or less evolved spirit transmitting information with its own agenda. Staying in the company of the most evolved spirit guides, angels and ancestors is always important, and if using divination, this is even more important. After all, divine-ation should be done in the presence of the Divine.

If one is a practitioner of divination, it is useful to develop the spirit of discernment. The diviner should be able to discern what energies or spirits are with the person being read. By doing so, the diviner gains further insight for the reading.

This question of discernment is interesting. If a person can discern, then why do they need the tools of divination? In fact, they ultimately do not need any tools, unless Spirit specifically instructs them to use a tool. This concept requires further explanation.

Divination has been used by many as a way to get started. They sincerely desired to hear from Spirit, and divination provided the easiest tool available. However, the time comes when the training wheels must come off the bicycle. Each and every person has the ability to see the past, and predict the future. Each and every person can discover truth within. Being bound by any tool, or exterior energy, is not the ultimate from of development. It is good to be weaned off mother's milk, and start to eat solid food.

The truth that is spoken here is recognized by those who use divination on a regular basis. Diviners have all seen their psychic or prophetic abilities improve as they have used the tools of divination. So the question is, will you trust Spirt within? When will you move to a new level? It might be shaky at first. You may not be as thorough or accurate at first, but in time you will be increased. Ultimately, there will come a time when you can choose to use divination not because you must do so to receive information, but because you are directed to do so by the Most High Spirit within. Being led by the Spirit is always the correct way to move. A way that will always insure accuracy in every experience you have.

Experience is another grand way Spirit speaks to us. Have you ever noticed there is a commonality about the experiences of spiritual masters like the Iroquois Peace Maker, Jesus, or Buddha? Spiritual masters always experience everything they truly desire. They have loving relationships, and companions all around them, ready to

41

bend over backwards at their slightest request. They have every physical thing they need. Everything they touch seems to work. Complete fulfillment and satisfaction is derived from every activity. Joy and happiness follows them everywhere they go. This is the way of Spirit within and without saying to the master, job well done.

The master's experience of life is a reflection of perfect communication and communion with Spirit. In fact, the word "experience" can be used to summarize this entire section on how Spirit communicates with us. Every experience, every person, every situation, every dream, every vision, every spiritual encounter is part of a grand scheme to give you the experience of Spirit. For Spirit is the All In All, and all that is experienced is Spirit in action.

The world you experience is a reflection of what you put out and create. This concept is discussed in great detail in the chapter on Stress, the SOS of Life.

Actually, experience is the definitive language of Spirit. Language is defined as a verbal or nonverbal method of communication. Communication is defined in the dictionary as: to make known; to manifest; to clearly reveal information. For example, the best way for Spirit to reveal clearly how its abundance works, is to communicate it to you by letting you experience abundance. By allowing you to experience the perfect manifestation of Spirit, Spirit is communicating to you its nature. As Spirit's nature is communicated to you, you begin to remember the perfect being you are. It is like a person with amnesia beginning to remember who they are upon returning to a familiar environment.

If we take this concept of using experience to communicate, we can begin to understand how a very highly evolved form of spiritual communication works. One spiritual being can literally throw a complete experience to another, like throwing a ball of energy. Upon doing so, the recipient lives through and experiences exactly

42

what the first threw. This is real interactive communication. Until we are advanced in Spirit, our consciousness may not recall this.

We learn with the spiritual experiences we have, like astral projection or distant seeing. As we experience, we remember who we are, and what Spirit is relative to us. Without the possibility of these interactive spiritual experiences we would be seriously hampered.

Spirit also uses experiences in our physical reality to communicate with us its divine nature, which is our divine nature. One of the most miraculous and intricate ways that Spirit uses physical experiences to speak to us is thought synchronizing events (synchronicity). This form of manifestation is so overlooked yet so important, that an entire chapter of this book is devoted to it.

How to speak to Spirit.

You can speak to Spirit in every conceivable way possible. You speak with words, thoughts, prayers, visualizations, dreams, goals, deeds, actions, relationships and created experiences. You are constantly and continuously speaking to Spirit. Everything you do and everything you are, is a statement to Spirit. For in reality Spirit is the All In All, and you are inseparable from this All In All.

The most profound and significant statement you can make to Spirit is simply to be. To consciously be what Spirit is. Not to try, not to do, but to be.

Talk to Spirit. Ask Spirit questions. Seek guidance from Spirit continuously. You do not have to get an answer immediately. Know in your heart you will be lead to the answers in the right time. However, do not develop a conversation of constantly begging or pleading for something. Allow Spirit to be your best friend and highest mentor. Be intimate and respectful in your conversations with Spirit. Be honest with Spirit in your conversations, because being honest with Spirit is being honest with yourself.

It is important to develop a consciousness of Spirit at all times. To understand this statement, think of an African woman walking tall carrying a water jug on her head. She is carrying on conversations, picking up the children, and involved in all sorts of activities while the water jug is perfectly balanced on her head.

Like this African lady, balance the energy of Spirit above, with the energy of the physical reality below. Be constantly conscious of angels, spirit guides and ancestors that are over your head guiding you, protecting you, and caring for you. At work or at play, walk tall and upright in Spirit, and never spill a drop of your precious cargo, the life giving waters of Spirit. Then have an attitude of gratitude. Constantly thank kind Spirit for its presence over your head.

As you open up to Spirit and begin to hear, be advised that you can open up to Divine voices, or the not so divine. A general rule is: you will be guided in truth, to the degree that you are truthful.

Spirit first taught me this lesson with another spiritually advanced friend. This friend was truly walking in spiritual arenas, but made a habit of telling big fish stories, or little white lies. This individual had a series of disturbing visions. As I listened to the visions, Spirit gave me a clear interpretation. However, my friend had a completely different destructive interpretation. My friend would not accept my interpretation. Then Spirit told me: "one is guided in truth, as much as one is truthful."

What you put out, comes back to you. You reap what you sow. If you put out lies. Lies come back. If you put out virtue, virtue comes back. This is a universal law that we are bound by in the world of relativity. In order to attract divine spiritual guides, and hear Spirit in a way that will allow you to awaken to your Higher Nature, you must always put forth truth. Speak truth to yourself, others and Spirit all of the time. For in oneness all is revealed. There are no lies. There is no hiding. There is only perfect, absolute truth.

There are many ways to speak truth. One of the most important ways to speak truth is through deeds and actions. When you do the things that align yourself with Spirit, a clear message is sent to the Universe that you are seriously seeking to walk in harmony with the All In All. This clear message is always answered. It is a spiritual law of amplification. The energy from your harmonious deeds are amplified, just as physics states that two harmonious waves of energy are amplified as one. So when one has deeds of honesty, integrity and love the Universe mirrors back honesty, integrity and love, and as one continues to act in honesty, integrity and love, these virtues are amplified within the person. Speaking truth with your deeds is an act of being one with the All In All.

The topic of speaking to Spirit is so vast volumes of books could be written on this subject, and not do justice to it. So in the limited space available, we will only look at a selected topic on prayer, and the power of thoughts and words. Prayer is a good place to start.

Prayer is something we do. Prayer is our intention. Every thought, word or deed we engage in is our prayer to the Universe, even if we do not realize this.

There is so much that can be written about prayer. This book could not possibly contain all of the topics. Let's start the discussion on prayer using the traditional definition, which is to acknowledge, appeal to, and connect with the Source within and without for the act of manifesting. For this guide book, the act of intentional prayer may take many forms, from spoken words, to images in visualization.

Two seemingly diametrically opposed views exist about praying for and manifesting things and issues. The first view says if you spend your time and energy in meditation and prayer to develop an intimate relationship with Spirit, prosperity will come naturally. This view goes on to say, stop praying for issues and things. It is a waste of precious energy to try to manifest through visualization, imagery and prayer everything you desire in life. We often desire more money, better relationships, new material things, and so forth. In fact, it is believed the more you get, the more you want. Reducing Spirit to being your supernatural manufacturing factory, to get the physical stuff you want, is like using the Hope Diamond to crack nuts. The nuts might crack, but there is certainly a better use for this diamond. It is easy for a person to waste their entire life acquiring things, and miss an opportunity of eternal life in bliss.

The second view says we are co-creators with God. It is an opportunity and our right to manifest everything we desire. Prosperity, loving relationships, fulfilling work are all things we should pray for, visualize and create right now. In fact, as we exercise our manifesting energy we become better at the art of creating. We should seize every opportunity at hand to manifest. It is what Spirit would have us to do.

So which view on prayer is correct. Neither is correct alone. They are both correct together. A delicate balance must be reached in the correct season of your spiritual development as to when to manifest, and when to hold back. This is how it works.

There is a beautifully woven universal matrix. Mature spirits matriculate through this matrix in which all points are connected. All paths lead to the greater good. All things work in perfect synchronicity for prosperity's sake, joy, peace and love. When we are mature we matriculate this matrix with ease. However, when we are still young in Spirit, we cannot navigate this matrix due to fear, and lack of faith. We fear that there will be lack, so we try to create wealth. We do not trust that loving relationships are our birth right, so we search high and low for a soul mate. We fear and believe we are being disrespected, so we get angry or depressed in response to the actions of others. Fear and lack of faith derails us from this matrix.

Understanding your ability to navigate this matrix determines how you should approach the manifesting game. If you are a beginner, it is best to use your energy learning how to maneuver in this matrix. This means spending most of your energy in prayer and meditation with the intent of developing an intimate relationship with Spirit. The following instructions show how to do this, and how to navigate this matrix.

First, decide what you desire from spiritual development. If you want to develop a personal relationship with the Most High Spirit within and without, and you want to awaken to your Higher Nature, True Self or Christ Consciousness, then you are on the right track.

Next, if you are still a neophyte in the spiritual arena, you must be able to admit you really don't know what is best for your spiritual growth. It is like a first grader going to school and telling the teacher what books to use, and what they should learn. This is ludicrous. It is just as ludicrous for you in your limited ego driven fear based mind to tell Spirit what you need. It may not be profitable for you at this stage of development to spend a lot of energy praying for issues and things. If you are a beginner you might wish to spend most of your prayer energy eliminating fear, cultivating faith, dying to your ego driven will that separates you, and praying for wisdom and love. This is the quickest way to awaken to Spirit, and navigate the universal matrix.

So how can you tell if you are a beginner? You may still be a beginner: If you still routinely give yourself to anger, depression, frustration or jealousy; if you still doubt the divine order of life, and choose to blame others for your life's conditions; if you are still hiding behind little lies like, "tell them I am not home" when the telephone rings, and you intellectually know in Spirit there are no secrets; and if a constant sense of being in Spirit every moment of life has not permeated your soul.

You are, however, mature in Spirit when you: can feel tearful compassion for a stranger's sorrow; rejoice over a friend's success just as if it were your own; no longer feel the need to tell little white lies; no longer give yourself to fits of anger or depression; can have dreams, visions and clairvoyant knowings as part of your daily life; see your words manifesting into reality in less and less time; feel the love of Spirit envelop, caress, and console you; can sincerely take responsibility for every thing that happens to you; know you are moving toward taking responsibility for all mankind's horrors; truly proclaim in your heart of hearts that you are walking with Spirit each and every moment of life, and your thoughts are no longer those of man, but of Spirit.

When you have arrived at this mature place in Spirit, your thoughts and desires no longer emanate from low level ego driven masculine energy, or fear based past experiences. Your thoughts are

48

clearly being derived from your Higher Nature and Spirit. You will know when to pray and manifest, and when to rest in Spirit. You will be in a place to easily create, receive and enjoy all things, while simultaneously wanting for nothing. It will be your nature to manifest in perfect harmony for the good of all. You will walk in perfect synchronicity, navigating the cosmic matrix of love and prosperity.

An advanced student or master in Spirit understands the true nature of prayer. Prayer is what you are. Your every thought, word, conversation, deed and action is your prayer. Prayer is a statement of what is. For as one is imbued with the Spirit, all things are possible. Words, thoughts and visualization instantly manifest into reality. In this state of instant manifestation there is no difference between the prayer and reality. Thus, a prayer is a statement of truth.

Obviously, there is a medium between the beginner and advanced student. On one's path to awakening, one must truthfully access where one is. Ask Spirit for discernment in this matter, and trust the answer can be revealed from any source, an unction, at work, a thought, a casual conversation, or a television commercial. Then strike a delicate balance as to what you pray for and manifest. The best rule of thumb is to listen to Spirit for guidance, and always choose to manifest in love. Let it be clear this discussion is about praying for exterior issues and things. For it is always appropriate to seek internal perfection.

Additional advice for when one is in between a beginner and master is as follows. It is important to remember Spirit within and without knows your needs. Praying by repetitively pleading and begging can be a sign of a lack of faith. When one prays with a lack of faith, then their prayer or visualization is really saying, I do not believe it will be manifested, and it usually is not. Also praying for a thing, and then worrying about it after praying, is a statement to the universe that I doubt I will get what I ask for. So you often do not get it. You must pray for a thing, and then release it.

Therefore the question is, how does one learn how to release it? The key is to find peace. When you can have peace of mind regardless of what the outcome is, then you can release it. (This concept of peace is discussed in detail in the section on 'Finding internal peace' in the chapter on Stress.)

Being between a beginner and master, one may not always be able to divorce oneself from the outcome. So you are urged to stop praying for every single issue in your life. Everything is in divine order, and everything is happening for a reason, so go with the flow.

Stop trying to deliver yourself from every perceived negative circumstance with prayer and visualization. A circumstance might just have been created by you to expose an unevolved quality within. Simply observe what is happening, and be resolved to change with the help of Spirit. The concept is to evolve to a point in which you can trust Spirit to bring you to the realization of when to manifest a thing. This is the art of navigating the matrix.

If you find yourself in a pressing dilemma and wish to pray for an issue, but you are not sure of the divine flow, there is something you can do. Simply hold everyone and everything in the Light. To make this point clear a true story will be shared.

The rental house burned to the ground. The fire investigation said the cause was a lit cigarette in the center of a bed.

The tenant was irate. She had no renter's insurance, and she lost every possession she had in life. She insisted that one of the repair men that had previously been at the house caused the fire. So she went to the fire marshal and demanded a full scale investigation. She was preparing to sue.

In the course of the investigation the insurance company would not pay. I had to continue to pay a $500 monthly mortgage with no rental income. Additionally the insurance company held up $20,000 I was to receive from equity. The tenant's irrational actions were costing me seriously.

The insurance company advised me not to talk to this lady under any circumstances. The matter must be solved in court. As I searched within, I did not understand why this was happening. I wanted it to be resolved, but I did not know the will of Spirit, or the divine purpose. So I chose not to pray for her to stop the investigation. Instead I did a visualization and pulled her image and essence up. Then I held her in the light with the intent of having her receive all the divine light and love she needs in life to be fulfilled. Then I pulled up myself, and did the same. As I came out of the meditation, I received a powerful knowing from Spirit, go see her. But I had been told by the insurance company not to talk to her under any circumstances.

The next day I found myself knocking at her door. When she opened the door I said, "I know you lost everything, and if I can be of any help, just let me know'. She invited me in, and we talked. She shared with me that the few items of clothes that did not burn had smoke damage. This bothered her daughter who had bad asthma, so she had to throw these items away also.

I then began to tell her meditation could help her daughter's asthma. And as synchronicity would have it, I had an introductory meditation class on tape in my car. I gave it to her, and left.

Two day later she called. She informed me that as soon as I left she listened to the tape. In a meditative state she saw the same three numbers twice. So she immediately went out an played the Georgia daily pick three lottery, and she won.

She went on to say, when she won this money, she started to realize God would provide for her needs. She also said she considered herself a Christian, and what she was doing was not right. So she was going to stop the investigation, and drop the suit. Within weeks I received the $20,000 insurance money.

If you feel a desire to pray for an issue, and you have not received from Spirit how you should pray, simply hold it in love and light. Then hold on, and ride the wave of the divine universal matrix of synchronicity to victory. Beware, never sabotage yourself by engaging in the use of self defeating words, and dwelling on limiting thoughts.

Thoughts and words are emissions of energy that have creative potential. This potential can be clearly understood by looking at an example of how electrical energy works.

In general, if electricity is organized it can be the source to emit other forms of energy. Radio waves, TV waves, microwaves, X rays and infra red are just a few forms of energy that are emitted into the air because there was a highly organized electrical energy source. In addition to these, new emitted energies are being scientifically discovered every year.

One class of rays or energy emissions that has not yet been discovered or measured by science is the spiritual rays that emanate from the highly organized complex array of electric current going through the human brain-mind. This electrical current can be monitored by numerous types of instruments. It is called by scientists the action potential. Spiritual rays are emitted from the complex array of action potentials.

This is more than a suggestion. Theoretical physics have predicted the existence of an emitted type of spiritual energy using mathematical formulation. Scientists are currently contemplating on how to discover this energy form.

This discovery process can be arrogant, and often as ludicrous as Columbus discovering America. How could Columbus discover something that was inhabited by the Native Americans for thousands of years?

All spiritual traditions throughout history testify to the existence of spiritual energy, and the power of thought to create. How can scientists discover this? All science can do is find a way to measure it with instrumentation. Science can only confirm what Spirit proclaims.

There are many who choose to be arrogant and short sighted, just like western science and history. They have chosen to believe that their thoughts are not powerful forms of energy that create, energy forms that are as sharp as two edged swords, which would be wise to monitor, control, discipline and train.

There are also many who testify they believe the power of thought, but it is only in their head, and not in their hearts. If they believed in their hearts, and truly understood the consequence of thoughts, they would treat thought differently. They would guard and safeguard every thought, just as they would safeguard a deadly sword. They would only swing their sword to cut away the illusion of lack and separation from the Source. They would never swing their sword randomly, it might hurt, kill and destroy. They would never consider swinging their sword in anger or frustration, for surely it would be devastating. Are you one of those short sighted people who choose not to believe in your heart the power of thoughts? I pray not.

Thoughts are powerful weapons of destruction, or peace. They are transmitted to, and received from, the universe. Words are manifest from thought, and amplify the power of thoughts. When the energy of thoughts or words are emitted into the universe, the universe receives it, and aligns itself in accordance. It is like placing a magnet under a piece of paper with iron shavings on it. The iron shavings arrange themselves in a pattern according to the magnetic emissions.

As the universe organizes itself according to our thoughts, we create a world around us. So, if we have thoughts of discord and mayhem, fear and stress, our world aligns itself accordingly to mimic our thoughts, just like the iron shaving mimics the magnetic emissions.

However, if we have thoughts of love, peace, harmony, and

abundance, the world aligns itself accordingly. We then have reflected back to us a world of love, peace, harmony and abundance.

There is another extremely powerful and interesting concept here. This concept can be best explained by looking at science again. A general principle of physics is that any wave of energy that moves in harmony with another wave is amplified. Everything in the universe is really nothing but energy. Love and hate, peace and stress, harmony and disharmony, matter and antimatter are all forms of energy. The nature of energy that exists in the Most High Spirit are the frequencies of love, peace, harmony and abundance. Therefore if you chose to think thoughts of love, peace, harmony and abundance, your energy waves will align with the energy waves of Universal Consciousness, and be amplified. Thus, the love you put out will ultimately return multi-fold in your life. In fact, its return will be infinite.

This concept of amplification parallels the spiritual traditions throughout the ages. The ancients have always stated that as we worship God, praise God, and seek righteousness, we will receive the fruits of Spirit, and go to heaven. It was understood that thoughts and words of worship, praise and righteousness would align one with the higher vibrations of the Universe. Doing so would ultimately amplify their love, peace and prosperity. Hence, catapulting their consciousness into heavenly states of bliss, and creating in their world the fruits of the Spirit.

It is up to you. The energy of your thoughts and words will be reflected and amplified back to you. Whatever you choose, the universe will oblige you. You can choose to hold on to your thoughts of confusion, frustration and victimization. You can choose to live in a world of competition and aggression by thinking this is what is needed to be successful. You can feel it is too hard to look at your thoughts, and choose to be lazy instead. You can choose not to look at your thoughts, because this might hurt your self-esteem or self-image. You can even choose not to listen to this warning. If you do, and as long as you do, you will reap the consequences, you will live in: a world of ups and downs, win one day, and lose the next; a world of turmoil, disappointment and unfulfillment; a world of deception, lack and oppression; a world of pure hell.

It is your choice. You have free will. No one can instruct you as to what thoughts and words to choose, and call your own. However, I can tell you what I choose and affirm. Hopefully, this will inspire you.

I choose thoughts of love. For I am love. I see all people as divine creations of Spirit, and I love them right where they are. No circumstance justifies fear or hatred. I choose to totally open myself to experience unconditional love, and I do experience unconditional love.

I choose thoughts of wisdom and understanding. For I Am Wisdom and Understanding. I live in the counsel of Spirit. Ignorance and misunderstanding does not plague my being, or stop my awakening. I choose to be still and hear Truth.

I choose thoughts of peace. For I Am Peace. I know my inherent nature is peace. No stress or press is large enough to rob my serenity. I choose to walk and talk harmony with all creation.

I choose thoughts of joy. For I Am Joy. I live my life in one big play ground. Sadness cannot penetrate my world. I choose to have fun and enjoy whatever I do.

I choose thoughts of gratitude. For I Am grateful. I give thanks, for all things are in divine order. Nothing can happen to me, that I can not appreciate. I choose to be grateful for the sacred gift of life.

I choose thoughts of forgiveness. For I Am Forgiving. I experience the forgiving nature of Spirit. No person or thing is so bad that I cannot find forgiveness in my heart. I choose to forgive and release all as a way of life.

I choose thoughts of patience. For I Am Patient. I remember the eternal timeless nature of my essence. No event or person can cause me anxiety. I choose to spend each moment of waiting in communion with Spirit.

I choose thoughts of prosperity. For I Am Prosperous. I have abundance on all levels of my existence. Scarcity and lack does not enter my consciousness. I choose to live in such great abundance that I have no needs.

I choose thoughts of generosity. For I Am Generous. I am freely given all, and I freely give all. Self centered selfishness is not in my world. I choose to freely supply all that is asked of me for righteousness sake.

I choose thoughts of humility. For I Am Humble. I am submissive to the voice and call of Spirit. Nothing in me calls for arrogance or egotistical thoughts. I choose to serve mankind with dominion and not domination.

I choose thoughts of honesty. For I Am Honest. I move in righteousness. No force can shake my integrity. I choose to be ethical, honorable, trustworthy and virtuous in all that I do.

I choose thoughts of perfection. For I Am Perfect. I know my path of awakening leads me to perfection. Nothing can deter me from this path. I choose to stay focused at all times on the quest to remember the perfect whole being that I am.

I choose thoughts of acceptance. I Am Accepted. I accept all things as the divine creation of the Most High Spirit. Nothing that is good, loving and whole rejects me. I choose to accept love, wisdom, peace, joy, gratitude, forgiveness, patience, prosperity, generosity, humility, perfection, honesty and Spirit.

I choose the thoughts of Spirit. I choose eternal bliss for my soul. I choose to be one with all that is good. I choose to be one with the Most High Spirit. For I am that I Am.

56

As you choose the most high thoughts you can conceive and believe, month after month, year after year, decade after decade, your world is slowly transformed by Spirit within and without. So declare to the Universe, "I am that I Am."

I am can be one of the most powerful affirmations possible. For it can be a declaration to the Universe your state of being. Nothing is needed to follow I am. Alone it is a statement of perfect being. A statement that the soul longs to hear.

The I am that I am statement, with intention can be the ultimate affirmation to the soul. Moses symbolically heard a great force upon a burning bush. It identified itself as I am that I am. If this affirmation is said with understanding, it is saying I am (you are) that great and powerful Spirit that the Most High is. I am (you are) that perfect energy burning without destroying. I am (you are) that same pure essence of love and beauty that you the Most High Spirit is. I am that I Am, and that is all I am.

What you put behind the I am determines the power of this affirmation. If you say, I am an electrician, doctor or janitor, you are diminishing your state of being. These statements are actually states of doing. These are statements of the body and mind. The body and mind involves itself in doing, the soul in being. However, if you declare to the Universe, I am love, I am joy, I am peace, I am an eternal immortal being of light. I am that I Am. Then you are identifying with a greater vibration, and your very feminine receptive soul flourishes.

Thank you kind Sprit.
For I am what you say I am.
I open myself to all that you are.
I release and die to my limited will.
I receive your holy and complete will.
I am yours, and you are mine. For we are one.

Common Sense Exercise: Journaling.

Begin a diary. Journaling daily or regularly is one of the most powerful tools for spiritual growth. Journaling is like a mirror for the soul and spirit. It reflects how you look within. It also reflects your history, and it may forecast your future. The act of writing ignites something in your consciousness. It lets your soul and Spirit know you are serious about this spiritual journey. With any serious attempt to grow, Spirit responds. As you make writing a part of your life, you might just be surprised at what comes through you.

Starting a diary is simple. In selecting a journal to write in, develop a system that will work for years. The goal is years from now you can go back and easily recapture a snapshot of your journey to Spirit. One method is to use a three ring binder with dividers. You can buy plain paper with holes at office supply stores. Date each written entry. When a section in your binder is full, remove that section to another three ring binder, date that binder, and store it.

Divide your journal into at least three sections. The first section should be on dreams.

The next section should be on significant spiritual events that happen to you. It is not necessary to write in this section daily. Only write about spiritual events like visions, intuitive knowings, prophetic readings, synchronicities, signs and wonders. At first, you may not have any events to record. That's ok, be patient. As the years go by, you will be surprised at how many entries will accumulate. Writing these entries helps validate the importance of Spirit in your life. This will result in your ability to hold the energy and blessings of these events. Reviewing this section over the years will bring into focus how everything is in divine order. Seeing this happen in your life is

58

extremely important for your belief system. This will increase your expectation, conviction and faith.

The third section is on your life in general. Write in this section significant emotional, or life changing events that happen to you, and how you respond to them. In time you will discover patterns of behavior. As you discover these patterns, you will uncover areas in your life which need work. You may add entries in this section daily, monthly or when events worth recording occur.

Thank you kind Spirit.

Chapter 3

Meditation

How to make meditation a way a life.

The universe opened up with a joy of anticipation. I saw a light of love and compassion surrounding and embracing me. I was a child born again into the Spiritual essence of love. My nostrils were filled with the fragrance of celestial peace. In the midst of angels and beings of light, I rediscovered myself. I was a new creature in Spirit.

If people could give a passionate testimony like this about their first experience in meditation, making meditation a way of life would be easy. However, most peoples' testimony is, "nothing happened."

To evolve into an experience like the above, you must have celestial assistance. You must be open to receive this assistance from the Most High Spirit, your Higher Nature, the angels, ancestors or spirit guides. Assistance comes not only in words of advice, but knowings, moments of euphoria, and experiences of enchantment. Assistance enlightens in times of confusion, comforts in times of distress, strengthens in times of weakness, and loves in times of adversity. To receive this wisdom, love and power, you must be an open vessel. To be an open vessel, you must master the art of meditation.

Meditation is the ultimate process for awakening spiritually. The prefix of meditation (med) is found in the word "Medusa," which is a Greek feminine participle meaning "to rule." True meditation is a feminine act of receiving. When you let receiving from Spirit rule your life, you will remember who you are. If you let your mind rule your life, you will remain in a state of confusion, distress and adversity. This is because the mind of a man is limited. It operates in fear, and has false ambitions. It makes decisions based on a narrow spectrum of past experiences, and it worries about the future. It finds its foundation in the collective consciousness of mankind, which openly accepts wars, senseless persecution and widespread famine.

When I first learned about the limitations of man's mind and the power of meditation, I was so excited I could hardly contain myself. I had finally found what I had wanted for so long. I knew meditation would change my life. It was like finding a genie in the bottle.

I took my first free introductory class on meditation while I was still in graduate school, and living on a budget of $300 a month. I did not have the money for the full class, so I went to every free introduction class on meditation I could find. When I finally graduated from school, I knew my time had come. With enthusiasm and excitement, I took several meditation classes. The first months after taking the classes, I meditated with passion and anticipation every day. But as the months went by, my daily, joyful meditation rituals, turned into weekly efforts. The thrill was dwindling bit-by-bit, like a slowly deflating tire. It became increasingly difficult to find the time to meditate in my increasingly hectic schedule. Eventually, I stopped all together.

Sadly, the majority of people who have learned the fundamentals of meditation do not meditate regularly, and eventually stop all together. This statement is probably even true of you.

So, the question arises, why not keep up a technique that is so beneficial to body, mind and spirit; a technique that has been scientifically documented to lessen stress, decrease biological age, improve health and sharpen mental capacities; a process that opens energy centers, leads to one's True Self, and connects one to the very source of the universe?

The reason is simple. People are always looking for immediate results. With meditation, fast results are not always evident, although results are present.

Meditation increases vibratory energy frequency and opens one up to Spirit in ways a person may not sense or appreciate immediately. This concept can be understood if you examine physical exercise as an example. If you decide to start an exercise program, finding the time each day is difficult. However, if you only exercise once or twice a week, months go by, and it seems like nothing has changed. The exercise routine is still strenuous and you have not lost weight. But if you can keep it up for a year, you will feel better, sleep better, and have more energy. In spite of this success, if you are like most people, the presses and stresses of life will eventually get you off your exercise schedule.

Meditation is much like physical exercise. If you decide to meditate for the first time, it is a struggle finding time in your busy day. And if you do meditate once or twice a week, and keep it up for months, it won't seem like anything has really changed. You won't feel any younger, healthier, smarter, or closer to the Creator. You may not have visions, out-of-body experiences or other spiritual realizations that some people talk about with great glee. But if you persevere, and meditate daily for at least a year, you will feel better, sleep better, and have more energy. Your days will just seem to be more harmonious. You may even be more in touch with your intuitive nature, and visions might occur. But again like exercise, if you are like most people, the presses and stresses of life will eventually get you off your meditation schedule.

When people stop meditating regularly, the same interesting story is told. "Things just don't seem to be working since I stopped meditating, or I don't know why I feel so out of sorts." People are often surprised when life seems laborious after they stopped meditating, because they never truly recognized life was getting easier for them when they were meditating. The changes are so subtle most people never realize them. Just as we change with age, the change in us is not always apparent until we reflect on how we were years before.

The key to getting off the roller coaster ride of meditating one month, and taking off the next, is to make meditation a way of life. Meditation must be such a part of your everyday existence, that not meditating would be like not breathing.

As meditation becomes a way of life, everything in your being testifies to peace, tranquility and harmony. Your normal awakening beta brain wave pattern starts to change to a uniform rhythmic alpha. You are in a constant mode of receiving wisdom, strength and power from within and without. Thus, this entire chapter is dedicated to teaching, motivating and explaining how to make meditation a way of life.

I was fortunate in my journey of making meditation a way of life. After my first class in meditation, when I was in my twenties, I continued to take many different classes. I joined formal and informal meditations groups. I worked on my fears and doubts. I never gave up looking passionately for that genie in a bottle. Now, even if I don't find the time to meditate, Spirit unctions me into this peaceful state. When this started to happen, I realized I had found that genie. However, the genie was not in a bottle, but within me. This same genie resides within you. The secret to releasing the genie within you is to rub the bottle with sincere passion.

Passion, as boundless enthusiasm, zeal and fervor is one of the most effective ways to help make meditation a way of life. Passion is a driving force humans can call upon to accomplish the impossible. Passion can resurrect a dead thing, and bring it back to life. Passion can move mountains and swim seas. If you use passion to make meditation a way of life, your journey into Spirit will be like a rocket shooting into the heavens.

Passion can be stimulated from various sources. For example, a woman was fighting with her husband every day and divorce seemed imminent. However, what she never expected was that he would sue her for custody of her only daughter. The stress of losing her husband, and feeling a failure as a wife was bad enough. But to lose her daughter, the one who made her life worth living, was unbearable. Her heart and soul were being torn apart. She felt that her life was being taken from her. In desperation and despair, she passionately turned to chanting and meditation two to three hours a day. This was the only thing she knew to escape the horror of the court case, and the taunting accusations that consumed her soul like a deadly disease.

The tragedy and distress lasted for more than a year, and she passionately continued to meditate. Then the unexpected manifested! She could see in Spirit. She became clairvoyant. The veil between the physical and spiritual worlds had lifted, and as a result, she became a professional psychic.

I have heard similar accounts of incidents many times in which a individuals passionately gave themselves to meditation because of a crisis. A divorce, death of a loved one, or life threatening illness propelled them to fervent prayer, and hours of daily meditation. As a result of their passionate search for peace, they were catapulted to another level of Spirit. It is not necessary to search for a dilemma, nor is it being implied for you to find a crisis, but to move into meditation with passion.

Imagine two people who independently decided to meditate at lunch. One person, while looking down at the floor, said apologetically to her colleagues in a monotone dry voice, "Well, I can't go to lunch with you today, I am going to meditate." The other person with a twinkle in her eye, and enthusiasm in her voice, proclaimed boldly to her colleagues, "I found an amazing new technique, that is going to change my life. It's meditation! I can't wait to get outside in the park and do it. Why don't you come with me. It's going to be fun. You'll love it!" Now, which of these two people do you think would have a better experience in meditation? Obviously, the second person.

Anything you do with passion and zeal will turn out better. The act of sustaining this passion e-motion (energy in motion) will launch you into altered states of reality, and allow the spirit of meditation to inhabit your being. As this happens, you become the meditation. Accomplishing this allows meditation to spontaneously become a way of life.

Another interesting thing happens when that wonderful e-motion called passion is used as a driving force to engage in meditation. Passion increases the number and intensity of supernatural experiences one has. It's like going to an emotional movie. You might just dream about it. As passion ignites new and exciting experiences, one's passion for meditation stays alive, and one's interest in meditation stays focused. Passion and meditation work together like a spiraling circle, constantly moving upwards.

Now let's consider what experts have to say about changing one's way of life. Psychologists state that changing one's behavior to incorporate something as a way of life, is a slow process. They report it takes two to three years of behavior modification, to invalidate the thoughts that caused you to behave the way you do. According to this train of thought, it would take two to three years to make meditation a way of life. However, psychologists also report that a habit can be formed in 30 days. Therefore, after three years of making meditation a way of life, you could stop in just 30 days.

Let's thank kind Spirit that behavior modification is not the only thing that factors into the equation of making meditation a way of life. Passion along with the flow of energy from Spirit, can change this whole scenario, and make meditation as natural as water flowing downstream.

Meditation is a natural flow. Meditation is playing mindless imagination games with your children. One can go into meditation while sitting silently on a bench on a busy downtown sidewalk in Manhattan. Meditation can be entered into during a drumming ceremony filled with shouts and dance, or in the midst of a hand clapping Sunday morning praise service in a Christian church.

Meditation is not to be a static ritual in which perfecting the exercise is the only goal. A meditation technique is anything that helps quiet the mind, find peace within, open your being to receive, and connects you to Spirit.

The most effective way to meditate is to flow with the energy of Spirit. In other words, start out with your regular ritual of prayer or meditation exercises, and move to other techniques as led by Spirit.

For instance, a woman named Joan was cleaning the house one Saturday morning, when all of a sudden an intense exhilaration of Spiritual joy fell upon her. Immediately she dropped her broom, and shouted out repeatedly "Thank you Spirit." As the energy increased she started pacing around the room and dancing. This lasted 20 minutes. Then instantly, an astounding peace enveloped her being. The peace was so profound she dropped to knees in silence. After about 10 minutes, she felt her breath flowing in and out, as if the very universe was breathing through her lungs. Her rhythmic breath inhaled Universal love, and exhaled the essence of her divine being. Then the visions started. As she journeyed through the universe, her guardian angels accompanied her. The meditation experience lasted over an hour.

The ultimate way to experience meditation is to go with the flow as Joan did. In general, women naturally will go with the flow. Men, on the other hand, must learn to be more open and natural. In any case, for Joan to do this, she had to be open to many different forms of meditation. In fact, she naturally went through five different mediation techniques before the visions started. First, she chanted

67

over and over again "Thank you, Spirit." Then she did a walking meditation by pacing the floor. This turned into dance, another form of active meditation. Next, she sat in silence, experiencing the peace. And finally she began the breathing exercise.

Be clear that the visions Joan received were not the objective or the hallmark to say the mediation was successful. Many people feel something like visions must happen for the meditation to be successful. Each stage of the process for Joan had its own purpose and was successful. The same is true for you, each time you enter into a meditative ritual or technique, know that it is successful.

There are many different meditation techniques, as well as descriptions, definitions and explanations of what meditation is. This is made clear from this example of Joan. In order to be clear on what meditation is and is not, three models for meditation are proposed.

The three models for meditation are: balance the mind, quiet the mind; and focus the mind. These models for meditation collectively describe and define the art of meditation. These models are not mutually exclusive.

As you gain an understanding of these models, you will see how all meditation philosophies and techniques fit within this paradigm. Understanding how all meditation techniques come together will illuminate confusion, especially when you take meditation classes that teach techniques which seem diametrically apposed.

The balance the mind model suggests there are three daily states of consciousness through which everyone naturally goes. The three states are awake, sleep, and drowsy. The first awake state is when the conscious mind is dominating over the subconscious mind. At this time you are awake, alert and in the beta wavelength (20 cycles/second) as seen on an electroencephalogram (EEG).

In the second state of sleep is when the subconscious mind symbolically dominates the conscious mind. At this time, the subconscious mind is in control and it does things like dream. This mind, however, is constantly vigilant. For example, one could be sleeping in the midst of the television running and children playing, but if someone were to knock gently at the front door the subconscious mind would wake up the conscious mind to deal with the visitor. Sleep is characterized by the theta (~5 cycles/second) and delta (less than 3.5 cycles/second) wavelengths.

The third and most interesting state is the drowsy state. This is when you are waking up, or going to sleep. Neither the conscious nor subconscious mind is dominating. This is a time when you can recall dreams better, and when you are more likely to have visions. This state is characterized by an EEG wavelength of 10 cycles/second, which is a number midway between the awake state of 20 cycles/second, and the deep sleep of 3 cycles/second.

This drowsy state is most interesting because it occurs at the same wavelength as meditation. The classic meditative state is said to be the alpha wavelength. The alpha wavelength is also 10 cycles/second. It is no accident that in the meditative state one is more likely to have visions than in the awake state. The meditative state is like the drowsy state, neither the conscious mind nor the subconscious mind is dominating. They are working together in tandem. You can enter a dream like state called visions, and be consciously aware of it.

So in essence, the model is saying when the conscious and subconscious minds are balanced, you are in the meditative state. This brings us to a very important concept. In the dozens of meditation classes I have taught over the years, I have heard countless numbers of people say, "I can not meditate." "I tried but I just can not get there." My response to them is. "Can you go to sleep? And can you wake up after going to sleep? If you can do this, you can meditate."

Everyone can meditate. This statement is so simple that many still choose not to believe it. Believe it, it's true. By choosing not to believe it, individuals constantly affirms they can not meditate, and they limit their experience by this negative affirmation.

The key to using the drowsy state to enter into a clear cut meditation is in learning how to hold this state without falling back to sleep or waking up. A simple exercise you can do is to get up around 4:00 a.m., sit up in the bed and practice your meditation technique. This is also a good time to meditate because the spiritual air is clean. Not many people are awake sending out conflicting spiritual energy into the air.

As one perfects holding the alpha wavelength in consciousness, one will eventually be ushered into slower more rhythmic patterns like theta and delta. When you are consciously awake at these slower wavelengths, your awareness resides more in Spirit. To illustrate this point: a lady in Georgia carried on regular conversations with the Virgin Mary. During one of these sessions she was attached to an EEG, and was found to be in the delta wavelength. However, according to science, a person cannot be consciously awake and talking in the deep sleep of delta. Well, so much for science.

Understand the balance the mind model is only a way to get a grasp on what meditation is. It is not a definitive statement of truth. It is a convenient way to understand meditation. As this model is comprehended, it opens the way to look at the second model for meditation: the quiet the mind model.

The quiet the mind model states one must quiet the internal dialog, chatter, and judgements of the mind to meditate. Quieting the mind is not something you can do. It is something you must be. Be quiet. Be silent. Be still.

Quiet the mind meditation techniques are methods that allow one to "be." To "be" in a receptive mode to receive Spirit.

70

True meditation is a feminine act of receiving. It is not a process of doing. If one moves into meditation with an agenda of doing something, it is not meditation, it is a prayer to manifest something. If one moves into meditation for the purpose of seeing or understanding something, it is not meditation, it is a prayer to receive. True meditation is a statement of being. True meditation has no agenda. It is not entered into to do anything except be. Be what you are, and in the process discover who you are.

Doing is not a process of be-coming. To be-come all you are in Spirit, requires be-ing, not doing. Doing something is a statement of the mind and body. You do work, and you do thinking. Everyone has used the common expression "I need to do some thinking." Meditation is the exact opposite of thinking. Meditation is not-thinking. Hence the quiet mind. This mental silence may be for a split second, or hours at a time.

The above explanation of meditation is not what people often think. People comprehend meditation as something one does; something like sitting in a lotus position with legs folded, hands on knees, and eyes shut for an hour each day; or doing techniques like imagery, visualization, and even self-hypnosis and hypnosis as forms of meditation. In the strictest sense, these are techniques of doing and not being. Now, that is all right. These are powerful techniques that need to be understood and done. But it is most important to understand the difference of doing, which is prayer, and being, which is true meditation.

To be, is not to think. Consequently, the biggest enemy of "the quiet the mind model" of mediation is thought. The brain mind is always thinking. It filters everything that comes through it, and the filter apparatus of this mind is thoughts. You are taught to think about, rationalize and judge every experience you have. Thus, our daily experience of reality is filtered and compartmentalized according to past experiences. This limited way of experiencing reality prevents spiritual evolution.

There is another way to perceive reality. This way is best understood by looking at a baby. A baby perceives reality directly without rationalization or judgement. A baby has no language to rationalize with, and has no past experience to judge against. A baby's mind is perfectly quiet, receiving reality directly just as it is. To understand this is to understand the scripture "a little child shall lead them" (Isaiah 11:6). In fact, small children's minds are consistently in an alpha wave length.

When your mind is perfectly quiet, you are open to receive reality just as it is. Spiritual reality comes not only in the form of thoughts, but visions, out-of-body experiences, altered states of consciousness, and heavenly states of bliss. If you drag along the logical mind that discriminates, you will rationalize yourself right out of these heavenly encounters.

Numerous meditation traditions focus most of their attention on trying to quiet the mind. But like an author humorously stated, quieting the mind is like trying to quiet a barrel of monkeys. To try to stop thinking just does not work for most people. As much as you might wish, most can't turn back the hands of time and return to infancy. You have responsibilities, plans, worries, fears and fantasies. You have grown accustomed to thinking continuously. To just stop thinking and give the mind a rest, to most people means falling asleep.

For this reason, many meditation techniques have been developed in which an object of focus is given in order to quiet the mind. This brings us to the third model for meditation: focus the mind.

The focus the mind model for meditation is brought into clarity by one of the several definitions for meditation in the dictionary, and is defined as follows: to concentrate, to contemplate, to focus one's attention. We are not referring to meditation by contemplating. The

72

ocus the mind model is a form of concentration in which one focuses on that quiet place, or balances the conscious, subconscious and uperconscious mind.

There are many ways to focus the conscious mind to stop it from thinking and dominating over the subconscious mind, soul and pirit. Techniques like chanting, mantras, visualization, physical movement, breathing and glossolalia are just a few. To understand how focusing the mind works in theory, let's examine the little understood, but widely used practice of glossolalia.

Glossolalia is defined as fabricated and meaningless speech, especially when associated with a trance state. Glossolalia can be spirit speaking through a person in another language, or it can be simple gibberish.

A Sufi mystic named Jabbar established the word gibberish. Jabbar taught thousands of his disciples the mind thinks with words. Eliminate the words with gibberish, and you will experience your being. Therefore, gibberish becomes the focus of the meditation.

The way to do this is to just start saying gibberish out loud. You may whisper, yell, chatter, cry or laugh, but do not stop vocalizing. Continue passionately making gibberish. Do it! Jump up and down, run around, or sit on the floor waving your arms. Be complete in the process. Do this five minutes to an hour, and you will have an amazing result. Silence will fall upon your being.

Glossolalia is one of the most powerful forms of focusing the mind techniques I know. I presently utilize this technique every day.

Are you wondering why you have never heard of glossolalia if it said to be one of the most widely used meditation techniques? Because a very narrow view of meditation has been taught in the past. In the Christian community, glossolalia is called speaking in tongues.

In many denominations of Christianity, speaking in tongues is a common and regular part of prayer. In fact, in some groups, speaking in tongues is considered a type of prayer. There are thousands of Christians who speak in tongues on a regular basis as part of their daily prayer life. In reality, it does not matter whether this technique of glossolalia is called prayer or meditation, the result is always the same.

In fairness to Christians, there are many diametrically opposed views about speaking in tongues. Many say it should only be done in a trance state induced by the Holy Spirit. In practice, most Christians speak in tongues, simply making gibberish, long before they experience the Holy Spirit descend upon them.

Understanding how glossolalia occupies the mind, and keeps it from thinking, can also help to see how chanting works. The conscious mind simply gets tired of hearing that some old thing over and over, and it shuts down. In addition, with chanting, certain mantras carry specific tonal vibrations which also assist in aligning one's energy for meditation.

It can generally be stated that any item one focuses on long enough to lure the conscious mine in a submissive state of receiving, and not thinking, has accomplished the task of quieting the mind, and creating the balanced state of mind.

After you have mastered focusing your mind and learned to effectively quiet the mind, this is when it all begins. Let it be said again, the goal is not to perfect these three models of meditation. The idea is simply to "be." As one be-comes, the universe opens up. The altered states of conscious realities appear. You may get caught up in various heavenly states of bliss. Communion with the angels and ancestors may occur. This is when the feminine Spirit of Wisdom ministers to your heart. This is when you experience being wrapped in the cosmic blanket of unconditional love, joy and peace. To experience the full measure of Spirit, one must experience the full power of meditation.

The full power of meditation is most often experienced when one does not pigeon hole meditation. One of the most common dilemmas is thinking the techniques one has learned are the best or most appropriate. This may not be true. There are literally hundreds of meditation techniques that help focus the mind.

It is strongly suggested that you take several different types of meditation classes, or read books from different traditions concerning meditation techniques. If you are attracted to a technique, use it long enough to make it a natural part of you. For example, breathing exercises initially feel very artificial. However, in time, this artificial breathing rhythm will feel very natural.

Sometimes you may know right away a technique is good for you, but often you may have to practice a technique for months or years before it feels right. There is a meditative zone that is reached with a particular technique, similar to the zone a musician or athlete reaches when engaging in their art. When you hit that zone, you know it.

The best way to know which techniques to try, books to read, or classes to take, is to let Spirit guide you. If it feels right, then learn it. Be warned however, do not let your preconceived ideas about meditation determine your feeling. Discern whether your feeling is coming from Spirit or your past experiences, teaching, and biases.

As you expose yourself to and learn various techniques, you will receive another advantage. You will be able to easily and naturally flow with different meditative practices in different spiritual seasons. (See Chapter 6 subsection on Spiritual Seasons.)

The spiritual seasons are important because as you evolve, and as the spiritual seasons change, what may have worked for you at one time, may not be as effective at another time. As you open up to the flow of Spirit, you will be led to the correct meditation techniques at the appropriate time.

Being led by Spirit is most important, because the ultimate teacher of meditation is within. The different classes on meditation is only to give your mind something to focus on until the ultimate awakens from within.

What these meditation techniques should do is help one receive Spirit. As one masters receiving, one is on the road to becoming one with the omnipotent Spirit. And as true mastery is reached, one will be able to speak, pray and walk 'in Spirit' with all power and wisdom.

When a master speaks 'in Spirit,' the physical and metaphysical universe within and without instantly changes. As you can begin to comprehend in your heart the true beauty, power and awesomeness of being 'in Spirit,' you shall be inspired to meditate even more. Fortunately, there is a beautiful encounter in Spirit that has enabled many to experience a type of instant manifestation. The experience is in lucid dreams.

A lucid dream is a dream in which your consciousness awakens in the dream state. It is a dream you can consciously manipulate. If you want to fly, you do it effortlessly. If you don't like the way the dream unfolded, you go back and do it again. In other words, your thoughts and words in a lucid dream have power, because your thoughts and words are alive in the lucid dream. If you have ever had a lucid dream, imagine living in a reality like this. Then add to this reality perfect harmony, love, bliss and oneness. It sounds like heaven. The more you move into Spirit, the more heaven materializes on earth. (Additional information is given on lucid dreams in Chapter 2 on dreams.)

Meditation helps you move into Spirit, because meditation helps you receive Spirit. Receiving Spirit is synonymous to be-coming one with Spirit.

Now let's examine the most appropriate way to use meditation to help us get in Spirit. Meditation is like listening to Spirit, and prayer or visualization is like speaking to Spirit. To appreciate this principle, it will be compared to a conversation with another person.

76

When you are in conversation with a person, it is foolish to always control the discussion with your opinion or agenda. You would never know what is on the mind and heart of the other person. You limit yourself to your own narrow thoughts and ways. Many people enter into meditation in this manner. They always have an agenda or opinion on what should happen. They use meditation techniques like visualization to fix something in their life, or help someone. These are important and noble things to do, and should be done. However, using meditation only in this way will never allow you to find out what is in the mind and heart of Spirit. You limit yourself to your own narrow world, never receiving Spirit, and never moving into Spirit.

This point is so important, it must again be said: Enter into meditation without an agenda. This is the way to awaken into your Higher Nature.

Your Higher Nature is who you really are on the inside, and the unfoldment of the supernatural world of Spirit takes place on the inside. This unfoldment is inhibited by the low level, ego driven masculine energy that loves to control. This energy comes from the mind of man. It must cease, and the feminine energy must awaken, because it is through this meditative feminine energy one receives.

A very important point on the side must be made now. Phrases like 'low level, masculine energy,' are used to capture the essence of the creative power of man's will to manifest confusion, mayhem and separation. It is to be understood that in oneness there is no high or low, greater than or less than, there is just one.

To learn how to completely live in Spirit you must make meditation a way of life. In the open feminine posture of meditation you can be taken into the heart of the Most High Spirit, and be awakened to the realization that this same heart is in you pumping life giving blood through your veins.

A way of life meditation exercises.

The dilemma is not to learn how to meditate, the dilemma is to make meditation a way of life. If you understand meditation as a holistic event that can be incorporated in almost everything you do, then making meditation a way of life becomes easy. The techniques presented here are ones you might not normally encounter in other classes. These techniques can be incorporated into your normal day's routine.

Most people are taught to approach meditation as a practice in which you set one hour aside each day and perform. This is problematic, because for most people their day is already filled with too many distractions. Trying to find another hour each day in your busy schedule can feel forced, and be stressful. A study of a group of theology students who were required to meditate each day showed less than satisfactory results. The results documented that finding the time to meditate became an object of stress.

Be clear, it is not being suggested that you not set aside time each day for ritualized prayer and meditation; it is suggested that you not get stressed about a daily routine. You will never be able to experience the true power of meditation if it is squeezed into a busy day. To discover the real power, meditation must flow naturally. It must be what you are, and not what you do.

If you incorporate the simple meditation exercises at the end of this chapter, you will discover something amazing. You will look forward to setting aside an hour or more each day to pray and meditate. And like the example with Joan, when you are unctioned (lead) into meditation, you will gladly stop what ever you are doing for the joy of Spirit that lies before you. This will happen because when you use the meditation exercises in this chapter to make your entire day a meditative journey, meditation will become what you are. As this happens your inner being will be constantly beckoning you back home.

The small number of meditation techniques presented in this guide book have been chosen for a particular reason: To empower you to make meditation a way of life. Most of these techniques will easily fit into a busy day, and can be incorporated into your normal schedule. Thus, if you do not get your daily one hour ritualistic prayer and meditation completed, you will still have the opportunity to meditate throughout the day.

A secondary agenda for including some of the techniques is to emphasize the diversity of methods that can be utilized to meditate. Do not limit your meditative experiences to the ones included in this guide book. Explore as many techniques as Spirit leads you to. Be creative. Watching the sun rise, setting on the bow of a sail boat gazing at the horizon, standing on a rock in the woods at night, are all beautiful expressions of meditation.

A word of advice, some techniques will work for different people better than others. For example, if you are an openly expressive, active person, and your life is characterized by movement and anxiety, then active meditations might be good for you. On the other hand if you are the unruffled type, slow and steady moving, then peaceful quiet and serene meditative techniques might be better for you. Be open. Try different techniques long enough to reap the benefits. This is especially important if you are led to a technique.

Rituals such as chanting are very good, and are not incorporated in this book. Take additional classes, read books and learn these and other techniques. Incorporate these methods into a daily ritual. For these techniques will represent the backbone of your meditative life. Whatever techniques you learn, strive to make meditation a way a life, every hour and every moment. Start with the moment you awaken.

Awakening meditations are extremely powerful for several reasons. You are still close to the balanced state of mind, because you are coming out of sleep. You are less in your busy thinking mind, and your body is rested and rejuvenated. At this time you can penetrate to your innermost core easily.

Also in the early mornings around 4:00 a.m., most of the world around you is sleep. Thus, the spiritual air is not cluttered with the thoughts of mankind. The air is peaceful, quiet and serene, a perfect environment for meditation. If you meditate around 6:00 to 7:00 a.m., a current of awakening energy from the millions of people living in your time zone is occurring. This is also a great time to meditate. You will literally catch the flow of this revitalizing awakening energy.

The greatest trap people fall into about morning meditations is feeling there is not enough time. There will never be enough time unless you want it to be. So decide that you want to get up ten to twenty minutes earlier. The trade off between a few extra minutes of sleep, and a few minutes of meditation will make a world of difference. If you make morning meditation part of your joy in life, joy in life will become a part of your daily experience.

It is strongly suggested that you do an awakening meditation every morning. The following three morning meditation exercises can be done before you get out of bed.

Wait and watch is a form of meditation which comes naturally. As soon as you wake up, sit up on the edge of the bed. Don't turn the lights on, don't put your slippers on, just immediately sit up and wait in silence. With eyes closed, go within. With anticipation and hope, wait and see what happens. The more often you do this exercise, the more you will feel, experience and see. This is a time of great beauty, peace and visions. Expect the unexpected.

Sit for at least ten minutes. If you are one that will not fall back to sleep, you may choose to remain on your back.

This exercise is best done when you awake naturally without the alarm clock. If you have set the clock, try holding in your consciousness when you go to sleep that you will wake up ten minutes before the clock rings. Most people can do this after several attempts.

Morning breath is a breathing meditation exercise that can be done as soon as you wake up. Upon awaking, stay in the bed, sit up with your back straight, or lie on your back. Breathe in deeply through the nose, gently expanding the abdomen. Hold it for a moment, and breath out very slowly though the mouth. As you do this breath exercise, focus your entire attention on breathing, and find your natural, divine rhythm of life. Do this for at least ten minutes and then experience the divine peace for as long as you can.

Many people find coupling morning breath exercises with visualization quite rewarding. If you fall into this category, you might enjoy the Father-Mother breath meditation. As soon as you wake up, lie on your back, close your eyes, and do this exercise for 20 minutes. Breathe in very slowly and deeply while simultaneously envisioning the golden light of the early morning sun moving into the top of your head, through you, and out your feet. As this Father light moves through you, know that it is cleansing your being. Then exhale slowly, envisioning the color of the dark blue ocean waters at day break. Allow this royal, dark blue energy to move into your feet, through you, and emerge through the top of your head. Know that this tranquil feminine Mother energy will comfort you, relax you, and increase receptivity.

At the end of this breath exercise, bathe in the tranquil feeling that is upon you. Then thank kind Spirit for the cleansing, healing and receptivity that is growing within.

Writing meditation is a process where you open up and allow Spirit to channel information through you. It has been referred to as automatic writing. The intuitive feeling to pick up a pen and write happens most often in the morning. However, it may happen at

81

anytime. If you wake up, and a deep, subtle knowing inside says "write", or you feel a wealth of information waiting at the edge your consciousness, or Spirit simply tells you to pick up a pen, then be obedient. You may be surprised at what flows through you.

Be open for any type of expression. Words, symbols, pictures, drawings, maps, numbers and geometric figures have all been the result of meditative writing.

The best way to prepare for this event, if it should happen, is to have a journal or diary. To do this read the Common Sense Exercise in chapter two on Journaling. Then always keep your journal and a pen on the night stand besides your bed in arm's reach.

Day meditations are all around you. Open your heart and eyes and see them. During the day hundreds of opportunities present themselves for you to enter into communion with Spirit. Seize as many of these opportunities as you can. You will never shut down from the receptive mode. It will keep the channels open to Spirit. This will make the time you have set aside for dedicated prayer and meditation even more profound.

Bathing meditation is an exceptional way to enter into a beautifully receptive mode of healing self. Do this meditation when you are taking a shower or bath in the morning or evening. Feel the warm water caressing your body, while you gently message every corner of your exterior being. Receive the healing energies radiating out of your hands. Don't just coldly scrub your body clean, lovingly caress your being with light and love while you wash the exterior.

As you are bathing, take a moment to feel the wash clothe fondling your skin. Know that this is the universe making love to your being without and within. Experience the warm feeling of comfort which results from this exercise. Call the name of each part of your body you wash, and ask for healing energies from Spirit to enter that part, and make it whole. Then during the process receive and feel the energy as it moves through you.

82

This exercise will only add a few minutes to your bathing time. As you practice the motions of this exercise, you will be astonished with how in time you will feel the light of love and healing move through your body.

Greeting with peace is a simple meditative process that changes you and the person you greet. When you meet and greet someone during the day go within your mediative zone and feel peace for that person. When you see the person coming to you, go deep within yourself for a quick moment, and experience the fullest measure of peace possible. This simple process of feeing peace reconnects you to the peace and love of Spirit, and it alters the person greeted. Some will actually feel a shift that has occurred because of your feeling peace for them.

Breathing is beneficial when you feel the peace of the day slipping from you. When ever you feel stress, stop and sit for a moment to do this short breathing exercise. First perform a short prayer or visualization for peace. Then breathe in deeply through your nose, extending the abdomen for a count of four. Hold it seven seconds. Then breathe out of your mouth, with the tip of your tongue on the roof of your mouth, for a count of eight. Repeat this cycle eight times. Then give thanks for the peace that has come upon you.

It is recommended to do this exercise two to three times a day, especially at work. Once you have grown accustomed to this exercise, you will be surprised how it will refocus, calm and center you. In fact, it is recommended to do this exercise a few times a day, even if you are not stressed.

Sensing is a process of feeling your surroundings. This simple meditation can be done wherever you go. When you walk into a room, sense the spiritual air. Is it happy, sad, light or heavy? When you visit a friend's house, sense what you feel, and trust what you feel. As you walk into a park or wooded area, put up your imaginary antennas and feel. Can you feel the plant life? Can you feel growth in the spring, or the hibernation in the winter? Sensing may take a split moment, or you may focus for longer periods of time.

Expansion meditation is started by sitting in silence. Feel yourself expanding: twice your size, then filling the room, then expanding and encompassing the entire building you are in. Feel yourself swelling and surrounding all of Mother Earth, its forests and trees, its lakes and oceans. Feel the bliss of expansion as you begin to envelop the entire universe, becoming one with all that is. As you re-center yourself, thank Spirit in your heart for the experience of expansion.

Whenever you have time, sit and expand. You may take a few moments, or you may do it for hours. In time, you will get the hang of it.

Listening to music meditation can in and of itself slow down the brain wave patterns and have a calming effect. Ocean waves, rain or wind blowing is called white noise. White noise is meditative. Many tapes or CDS specifically designed for meditation have white noise incorporated into the background.

Purchase several good meditation CDS, preferably ones with white noises in the background. You can find large selections of meditation music at many metaphysical book stores. Play this soothing music continuously at home. If you can play it at work, let it create a spiritual meditative environment all day long. I have done this for years.

Using your meditation music when actively meditating will enhance the effect your music will have during the day. As you actively sit and meditate with your music, your mind will begin to associate this music with a peaceful state of being. This Pavlovian response will help create the meditative atmosphere during the day.

Daily walking any where can be turned into a meditation. The concept is simple. Whenever you have anywhere to walk that will take you over a minute, use this as a time to pray and meditate.

To get the full benefits of these walking meditations, it is suggested to engage in the walking meditation that is discussed in the Active Meditation section. If you do this longer walking meditation enough times you will eventually learn how to fall into a mediative zone. Once you have discovered this zone you will be able to hit this same zone when you are taking short walks. It's like typing. Once you learn how to do it, you can do it at any time.

Laughing meditation is literally a joyous meditation anyone can do anytime. When was the last time you had one of those gut busting, buckling over, hearty, long uncontrollable laughs. The kind of laugh in which your mind seems to go into a zone, and afterwards a feeling of calmness penetrates your being. Well, the last time you did this, was the last time you had a laughing meditation.

A laughing meditation can re-balance the body, mind and soul almost instantly. Have you ever been in an argument and something funny happens. The energy of the argument immediately disperses. Laughing is a miraculous form of meditation.

So obviously one may ask, "where is the meditation in laughter?" First, during laughter you are not thinking. Thoughts have been kicked to the curb. Your entire body, mind and soul is involved in positive convulsions of hysteric laughter. These convulsions radiate waves of uplifting energy through your entire being, energizing, balancing, and rejuvenating it. In fact, medical science states that smiling and laughter have measurable positive health benefits.

Second, the feeling of release or calmness after the laughter is another stage of meditation. This feeling of tranquility is somewhat similar to the sensation felt after any good meditation session.

Engaging in a laughing meditation is simple. Just let yourself be tickled. Don't hold back. Don't get embarrassed. Lose yourself in the laughter. At first when you give yourself to laughter it may be forced. But soon the sound of your exertion will cause authentic laughter. Authentic laughter is contagious, meaning others will join in. This is because a spiritual fragrance of laughter goes out into the room and tickles the nostrils of others. When this happens your laughing meditation becomes more profound because you have loosed the spirit of laughter in the air.

To release the spirit of laughter, be like a child. Children find humor in almost anything. A poke in the side, or a funny face will do. Find the child within, and you will find the spirit of laughter.

Laugh alone, or laugh with friends and family. Choose to do it as often as possible, and as long as possible. It can change the entire temperament of your day.

If you are in a spiritual group meeting, and the spirit of laughter hits a person, don't be so quick to end it. Go over and touch someone else on the shoulder while you are laughing. This is a sure way to get someone to join in the fun. Then keep on laughing, five, ten, twenty minutes or longer.

In your family, make laughter a part of your daily household experience. Grab every opportunity to laugh. Have fun. Laugh so long you forget what you were laughing about. Be sincere with your laughing, and your family members will have no choice but to join in. Then thank kind Spirit for your family's quality time in meditation.

Just plan fun meditations are what life is all about. Have fun. Engage in hobbies. Enjoy yourself, and make it a meditation.

Be creative. Find ways other than the following list to have fun and meditate. For as you experience the meditative zone while having fun, your consciousness will relate meditation and Spirit to pleasure. This will make it easier to make meditation a way of life.

Artistic hobbies that do not call for analytical or critical thinking may be meditative. For example, painting, drawing or even doodling can be a very significant form of Spirit expression. There is a lady who, in her spare time, would relax by doodling with a pencil on large pieces of papers. She saved them for years, and now people are buying them.

If you have an artistic hobby, and you feel you are receiving inspiration from Spirit, then be more cognizant of the process. Let it be a form of meditation.

Music Playing for accomplished musicians can be meditative, especially if they flow with creative, soothing music. Artists are advised, however, to also engage in other forms of meditation for balance.

Vacation meditation can be carried from the vacation resort to your everyday life. This exercise is to be done when you go on a vacation designed for rest.

Take with you only one meditation tape or CD. Play the same CD over and over again while you are on the vacation. Play the CD when you are relaxing in the sun by the beach, or walking through the forest at day break, or experiencing any great moment during the vacation. Play the tape in your car while you are driving. Take a walkman with ear phones, and play it as much as possible. Engage in as much passionate prayer and meditation as possible during the vacation, and play the tape during these times in Spirit. Allow this music to be the theme of your vacation.

On vacations, the heart rate slows, blood pressure decreases, and general health improves. By repeatedly playing the same tape on your vacation, your body will associate this music with this improved general health and well being.

When the vacation is over, and you play the tape, your body and soul will remember the relaxed state it experienced on the vacation, and automatically go there again. It is not necessary for you to mentally recall the vacation, just play the music. You may play it during your set aside time to meditate, or during the day. It does not matter, your body will remember.

Active meditations dynamically balance the body, mind and spirit with energy. It invigorates the body, and prepares it to be a sturdy vessel for receiving the energy and essence of Spirit. Some

87

form of activity or exercise is recommended for everyone. Why not make it a meditation?

Running or jogging can produce a profound meditative state. During running, blood actually increases to the right creative side of the brain, and endorphins calm the nervous system. These physiological changes prepare the mind to go into conscious-subconscious balanced state of awareness.

If you are a runner, swimmer or exerciser that does any type of repetitive movements, you may have experienced the awesomeness of this form of meditation. At some point, you become the exercise. Your entire body, mind and soul functions together, and amazingly, a profound peace explodes within.

Any solitary aerobic repetitive exercise can easily open the door to divine spiritual states of consciousness. These states are usually achieved if the exercise routine is significantly over twenty minutes.

Before engaging in the exercise, it is a good idea to say a prayer, or do a visualization, inviting the presence of Spirit. This also sets your intention to allow your exercise to be a meditative one.

While exercising, be mentally and physically as loose as possible. Avoid letting the exercise become so automatic that you start engaging in internal dialog about the day's events. Enter into the exercise to enjoy it, and not to beat yesterday's time. A mind set of competition could destroy a mind set of meditation.

Upon finishing the exercise, stand or sit upright with internal silence. Breathe deeply from the belly. Experience whatever is happening inside for as long as needed.

Walking meditations are for those who are not inclined to run. Walking is one of the best movements for balancing and rejuvenating the body, mind, spirit connection. Walking massages the lymphatic system, caresses the mental faculties, exercises the lungs and muscles. Walking soothes the soul.

There are many kinds of walking meditations. Reflective walks are when you reflect on life's events, and bring clarity to them. This meditation is best done when you make it a point to go to a serene environment like a park, lake side or ocean front. It is, however, suggested that this be a less frequent form of meditation you engage in. This meditation is more of a contemplation, unless you have established a clear channel of dialoging with Spirit. If you have such a channel, reflection comes along with instantaneous guidance from Spirit.

The empty-mind walk is a meditation that can be done on a regular basis. Simply walk and clear your mind of all your worries or concerns. Clear your mind by focusing on the walk, chanting while you walk, or marveling in silence at the beauty of Mother Earth. If you choose to chant during the walk, the chant you choose is not as important as the focus you engage in when you chant. Find a chant or mantra from classes, books or your spiritual tradition. Or be open to receive one from Spirit.

Glossolalia is another effective way to clear your mind while walking. However, if you choose to pray during your walk, let the prayers be an inspiration from Spirit. Do not engage in a wish list prayer session, or prayers that require thought.

A walk of at least 20 minutes is recommended. Longer walks for up to one hour are better. This meditation is strongly recommended to be done at least three times a week. Especially if you do no other form of exercise.

If your walk is brisk, it will have great cardiovascular benefits. If not brisk, it will still be a great meditation. Let Spirit lead you as to the pace.

Dancing, if you enjoy it, then this is the perfect meditation for you. Dance, jump, twirl and move with Spirit. You can play music, or you can do it in silence. The only key is let it be an inspiration, and not mechanical motions.

If you let it be an inspiration from Spirit, in time you become the dance. You will find you are no longer moving your body, but a greater force is moving it, deep down within your being.

I have seen a person hear an African drumming tape, and immediately do the African dances that were designed for each song. The person even called out the names of the dances. This individual had never heard this music before, seen the dances, or heard the names of the dances. This is the kind of dance you are to give yourself to.

Of course, most people will not do this at first. But everyone can incorporate the same principle this person used to do this. The principle is to be free in the dance. Let your body go. At first you may be controlling your movements, but in time you will be able to let go.

Dance to meditation music, gospel music, drums, recorded chants. Dance to the silence within. Dance slow, dance fast, it does not matter, but dance passionately. Do not engage in a repetitive learned motion unless Spirit unctions you there.

After finishing the dance, sit, stand, or lie down in silence. Allow everything in you to be still. Receive the Spirit of the moment.

This dancing meditation is not done best with contemporary music. Contemporary music has a spirit of its own. In most cases this is not the spirit you are looking for.

Evening meditation is a great time for communion with Spirit. In the evening you have finished all the tasks for that day. Your daily journey is coming to an end, and you have reached the destination point. It is a time of celebration and rest. See your evening thus, and celebrate the day's journey with prayer and meditation.

Ritualistic prayer and meditation for many people is done in the evening. In the evening you may choose to set aside time for your daily routine involving your personal faith, religion or philosophy.

90

Engage in it with a sense of joy, enthusiasm and anticipation. Avoid bringing a sense of duty. If you do it out of love for Spirit, the rewards will be great. If you do it out of a sense of requirement, the benefits will be diminished.

Rewind the recorder is a simple exercise to wind down your mind after a busy day. It can be done just before your evening prayer and meditation; however, it is best done just before going to bed. Many people who think too much or worry a lot upon going to bed find this technique helpful.

Start with a short, sincere prayer or affirmation thanking kind Spirit within and without for allowing the pressing events of the day to be diffused and released. Then begin thinking about the day's events chronologically from the morning to the evening. Quickly call to remembrance one at a time all major events of the day. Especially any events that were unresolved or stress causing. After you recall each event, say a short affirmation to release the event. For example you might say: "In Spirit, I release and let you go." Visualizing or feeling this release is also very powerful.

Do not engage in recalling great details of the day's events. This entire technique takes no more than several minutes. At the end of recalling the day's events, say another prayer or affirmation thanking Spirit within and without for the release of the day's events, and for the coming night of revitalization and growth in dream time.

This is a technique of doing. However this simple technique unwinds the mind similar to the type of dreams that defuse the day's events. By becoming proficient with this technique, the quality of dream time may improve. In addition, freeing the mind of the day's events opens you to "be."

In summary, now that you have exercises which go from the awakening hour to bed time, memorize these techniques. Start them today. By incorporating them into your life, you will be on your way to making meditation a way of life.

Remember, be patient with your expectations from your meditative way of life. No great feat is accomplished overnight. For some it may take a few years of daily passionate meditation before a significant change is noticed. A change in which you start to function in spiritual abilities and gifts. However, if you incorporate meditation into your everyday routine, there are almost guaranteed benefits that will occur in short measure. Your vibratory energy frequency will increase. Your biological age will start to decrease. Peace of mind will creep up upon you, and life will flow much easier. These things manifest, even if you don't notice it.

Another critical point that must be emphasized is to acknowledge Spirit in all of your meditations. Keeping an awareness of Spirit when you deliberately enter into and exit the feminine receptive posture of meditation is vital to your growth. For Spirit within and without will show you the way. In addition, holding in your consciousness at all times that you are a spiritual being having a human experience is critical to undeviating evolution.

While be-coming the daily meditations, do not forget to pray constantly throughout the day. This prayer can take the form of simple internal dialog with Spirit. Know that each and every thought and word uttered out of your being is a prayer. Intend that every thought, idea and feeling you receive comes from Spirit. As this becomes more and more your mind set, you will move closer and closer to your Higher Nature, a nature one with Spirit.

Thank you kind Spirit.

Chapter 4

Stress, the SOS of Life

How to make Suffering-Oppression-Sorrow (sos)
Saves-Our-Souls (SOS).

Why is there stress in life? Why do we suffer? What is pain all about? Is it really necessary? We have all asked these questions and the answer is simple. Suffering, oppression and sorrow (sos) are the soul's cry for growth. Once we understand the spiritual reason and potential benefits of stress, life becomes a little more bearable. In fact, stress can be one of the greatest spiritual gifts we have to save our souls (SOS). It is one of the most powerful internal monitors to keep us from straying from the spiritual path. In this chapter, you will discover how stress can save-our-souls.

Spirituality and stress are best understood by first laying a foundation about the nature of stress. Let's start by examining how stress occurs in cycles. Let's look at Harry.

Harry got up in the morning feeling great. He greeted his wife with a joyful "good morning." He was truly energized and ready for a fantastic day. However, enroute to work, he had to deal with the morning traffic, the same old complaining clients, an overly demanding boss, deadlines, and another lunch period cut short. At 3:00 p.m. his wife called, and asked how was his day going. He immediately barked "terrible." Then started to complain.

Harry is a typical example of how day-to-day stress can rob you of your positive state of mind. It is of paramount importance to understand how day-day stresses develop as cycles in our lives. The complaining, negative conversation, and worrying Harry got involved in, and we all have done, is a form of negative affirmation. Affirmations are self-fulfilling. What you affirm will soon be reality. When negative affirmations are said while in a stressed state, emotions are high. Emotions energize the negative affirmations. These energized negative affirmations aggressively attract to you what you have worried about. So a cycle has been created in our lives. We get stressed by the same daily events. We emotionally speak negatively about these events. This pulls these events to us and we continue to live in a state of confusion, despair and oppression, not understanding how to get out of the same stress every day.

In our fast paced, crowded, ever-changing society, stress has become a way of life. Hourly aggravations are cumulative within the anatomy of our body-mind-spirit. Consequently, these small aggravations eventually trigger themselves in a full blown, adrenalin pumping, muscle tensing, stress response. This day-day, year after year cycle eventually transforms itself into serious illness, spiritual dullness and early death.

It is a medical fact that stress drains the physical body of energy, and clouds the mind of clarity. Research has suggested as high as 90% of all illnesses are due directly or indirectly to stress. Mentally, a stressed person reacts out of fear, lack, and confusion. Anger, hatred, envy are all magnified during stress

The effect of stress on the body-mind has been exhausted in the literature by thousands of articles. But little press is given to the effects of stress on the soul and spirit. The Most High Spirit is harmony perfected, and stress is the complete opposite of harmony. So stress is like a thief in the night. It robs your soul of peace, joy and harmony. It deafens the spiritual ears, and blinds the third eye, making it difficult to receive from Spirit. Stress drains the spiritual life force from a person like pulling a stopper out of a sink of water. Stress lowers one's vibratory energy frequency. It transforms a brilliantly glowing aura into a dull chaotic energy field of irregularly pulsating light. One cannot channel the Creator's energy when the channel is full of holes caused by stress. The daily cycle of stress contracts the spirit, leaving it without love, the glue that holds the Universe together.

Now that it is very clear how stress occurs in cycles, let us continue the foundation information on stress. Let's look at when stress is damaging, and when it is healthy.

The damaging effects of stress result from an inappropriate response to one's reality. If a man in a rain forest is confronted by a wild panther, it would be appropriate to have a "fight or flight" response (this is the stress response). On the other hand, it would not be appropriate for the man to become reactionary, defensive, with jaw muscles clenched, eyes bulging and adrenalin pumping, because the car in front is moving too slow. If you can not fight or run, and you get upset, then it is inappropriate. Fighting, running or physical activity diffuses the stress response, and can be healthy.

The stress response is a mechanism to protect the physical body when it is threatened. However, people go into full blown stress responses when the physical body is not threatened. This occurs because of programmed beliefs and habitual thought patterns. Your body and subconscious mind do not differentiate between an event that is life threatening, and an event that just threatens or contradicts your beliefs. Let's look at one example. If you sincerely believe time is money, and hurrying has become a part of your life, then stress will result if something or someone slows you down.

The above concludes the classic textbook foundation about stress. We can now explore how the stress response can be a powerful monitor to save-our-souls. During the day, if you feel yourself starting to get caught up in the same old daily cycle of rushing, worrying or complaining, or you feel your heart racing, breathing rate increasing and muscles tensing, an alarm should go off

95

in your consciousness. You are getting stressed! You are straying from the spiritual path.

An internal alarm system can be developed to tell you when you have momentarily strayed from the spiritual path. With this alarm, you will have the opportunity to stay centered all day long. The choice will be yours. At the moment your alarm goes off, you can choose to get stressed, or grow spiritually.

This alarm technique can be implemented to monitor habitual patterns of stress related or induced behaviors. A classic example of a habitual pattern is rushing. Rushing is of particular importance; it is a chronic problem for most people. We rush to get to work, get the job done, and be productive. This internal sense of rush is damaging because it prevents one from hearing. The dilemma of rushing is painfully obvious if you have ever visited and spent time in a less technologically developed country. It is possible to move efficiently and be productive without rushing.

Other habitual patterns that may be considered are negative conversation, complaining, excessive talking, mood swings, worrying, and so on. So the first step in this technique is to become clear on the chronic behavior you want to address.

The next step is to turn the alarm on. The alarm is not an actual buzzing in your consciousness, but just an awareness that you are moving out of harmony. There are several ways to turn on the internal stress alarm. First, just hold in your consciousness that you will do this.

Second, visualize yourself immediately recognizing the beginning of a stress cycle. In your visualizations, see yourself about to engage in an inappropriate daily activity. Then see the alarm immediately going off. Do several short 30 second visualizations a day. Make sure in your visualizations you turn the alarm on at the beginning, before you actually get in a full blown stress response. This is very important because often during the day we do not even realize we are being stressed and pressed. It is our normal mode of operation. When we realize we are stressed, the damage has already occurred. We are tired, drained, and out of balance.

Obviously a more direct approach is to visualize not engaging in the stressful behavior at all. It would be prudent to do this. However, years of experience have demonstrated a back door approach: the alarm, is often required to break cycles of habitual patterns.

The third step is to implement a trigger response to the alarm. A trigger response is an affirmation or statement you say as soon as the alarm goes off. The trigger will help reverse the stress response. For example an extremely powerful trigger response is, "It's all in divine order."

Choose one or more trigger responses. Trigger responses are most powerful when they come out of your personal experiences. For example, one of the most powerful trigger responses for me is: "Walk not run." This personal trigger response is powerful for me, because when I first heard it, it rocked my soul. I was at a nine day spiritual retreat helping coordinate activities. As usual, I was rushing. I went to inform a Native American medicine man of a ceremony that was about to happen. I knocked on his door, told him, and proceeded to rapidly walk away. After the second or third step, I heard this resounding voice bellow out from behind the closed door: "Walk not run!" The power and command of the voice stopped me in my tracks. I immediately took a look at myself, and realized I had become stressed at one of the most powerful retreats I had ever attended. His words stuck with me. From that day on, I adopted that trigger response for whenever I am rushed.

Many people find inspiring scriptures to be great trigger responses. Ancient scriptures have been conferred by Spirit and used to inspire throughout the ages. They have a unique and powerful energy associated with them, an energy that was created by thousands of people saying them throughout antiquity. You may wish to choose a meaningful scripture as a trigger.

Upon implementing the alarm-trigger mechanism in your consciousness, there is another important concept to consider. You, and you alone, create and attract all of the negative stressful events that happen to you. You are the author of all of your suffering, oppression and sorrow, and these creations of yours are opportunities to bring you closer to Spirit.

You create your own stress is one of the most difficult points for people to accept on their spiritual journey. The origin of the pain, sorrow or suffering is not external events. Nor did God do it to you to teach you a lesson, or punish you. The origin is in us. Your world is a reflection of what is happening within you. Stressful circumstances happen in our lives because the spirit of those circumstances are within us. No, the devil did not do it to you. Nor did the devil make you do it. The devil is in you, and you attracted devilish things to you.

In our unawakened spiritual states, there still resides mental programs and energy frequencies that are not of love. As these dark forces are released from our being, they exude a spiritual fragrance that attracts the sharks of life. When the sharks come to kill, destroy and devour, we make the assumption we are victims of circumstances. And in our misery, we cry out, "why me." It is you, because you attracted it to you. And that's OK. It is part of the process of evolution.

This notion that we attract negative to us is a large pill for many to swallow. Why would someone decide to be financially strapped? Who would ever chose to be a victim of crime and violence? To understand this concept, there is much to consider; many separate points to understand. You must first understand time. Then second the world of duality; and finally, the process of rediscovering who you are.

The first point in understanding how we attract negative deals with time and the nature of our spirit. Our spirits were made before the heavens and earth were formed, and before time was.

This concept of being created before time is not far fetched. In fact, it makes sense if you contemplate it. Quantum physicists clearly tell us time and space is only an illusion of the physical world. In a reality called the space-time continuum, time and space do not exist as we know it. For example, mathematical calculations theorize that if you could fly fast enough, you could take off in a space ship, journey for ten years, and return home at the same time you left.

Our current scientific technology cannot make physical matter move this fast. However, science has identified and measured other subatomic particles and wave lengths which routinely move fast enough to defy time. These subatomic particles and energy vibrations must be the substance that our spirit and thoughts are made of. This would explain how psychic readings and prophecy is possible.

The mathematical model suggesting the existence of an infinite timeless reality is fundamentally supported by ancient scriptures. It is said God always was, and always will be. Our spirits are created in the image and likeness of God, the timeless Infinite Universe. Therefore, our spirits are also timeless. We have existed from the beginning of time, to the end of time. We were created before earth was formed.

So it stands to reason if we were created before the earth was made, and we are made in the likeness of God, we are also made in the image of perfect love. For God is love. The true essence of our spirits are created in the image of purity, love and oneness. In this state of original creation, we could only know love. We were perfect by design. We could only choose righteousness. This was our nature. There was no opposite to good.

This brings us to the second point to understand. Through birth in the earth plane, the crude and slow nature of physical matter refocused our spirit's attention from the timeless spiritual realm, to the physical world of time, limitations and relativity. The illusion of time, space and relativity quickly overwhelmed our consciousness, and like a kind of amnesia, we forgot our timeless perfect nature. By doing this we took it upon ourselves to experience the world of relativity or duality. In this world of duality evil exists along with good. Just as the symbolic story of Adam and Éve eating from the tree of the knowledge of good and evil, we also eat of this same tree. For this tree is symbolic of the world of duality.

From the perspective of duality we receive a different vantage point of who we are. It is one of the greatest opportunities the Universe could have ever given us. The world of duality is full of exciting new raw energies. A great adventure lies before us.

Now, let's examine the first and second points together in more detail. Man's spirit was made in absolute unconditional love and perfection. There was no opposite to this state of being. Consequently, man's spirit could not truly experience the awe of his perfection without comparing it to something. A world of duality or opposites was needed. Let's examine this point further. How can one truly experience the fullness of love, if one does not experience hate and fear? If one does not experience imperfection, how could one really appreciate perfection? Consequently, man could not truly experience the awe of our perfection without opposites to compare it to.

This point is made more obvious by looking at examples we can easily relate to. How could you know the joy of raising a child if you never had one? You can not. You have nothing to compare it with. If you are blind, how could you experience the joy of a sunrise? You can not. You need the opposite of blindness, which is sight. The same concept is true about perfect bliss.

Perfect bliss can only be fully experienced when the opposite of suffering, oppression and sorrow reflects it. This is why it is said that pain, sorrow and suffering comes as an opportunity to bring us closer to Spirit. Without journeying through the physical world of duality, we would be strangely doomed and inhibited from experiencing the full range of love, perfection and bliss.

A glorious part of the human journey is to experience good and evil. Up and down. It is a blessing to be able to experience the expanding, warm and comforting energy of love, and contrast it to the contracting energy of fear. To be able to choose between love and hate, because we have the faculty to do so, is a sacred gift.

Of course, many would not think that living in a world of good and evil is a sacred gift. They say when Adam and Eve ate of the tree of the knowledge of good and evil the Bible called it a curse. They were kicked out of the Garden of Eden. Yes, it was a curse. But if you look up the word curse in the American Heritage College dictionary, its first meaning is: "an appeal or prayer for evil or misfortune to befall someone or something." And this is exactly what happened.

When Adam and Eve symbolically ate of this tree of duality, they made an appeal for evil to befall them. We make the same appeal for evil to befall us by our very existence in the world of duality. Strangely enough our appeal for evil to befall us continues on each and every day. It is in the form of judgement, self condemnation, fear, hatred, anger, negative affirmations and limiting thoughts. These negative thoughts are timeless energy forms, and like fragrances, they go out into the Universe and attract back to us stressful events.

Without the world of duality serving as a mirror, we would not have the opportunity to discover experientially who we are. At first glance, this whole situation of us creating our own misery to experience perfection, seems tainted. However, there is a Christian saying which illuminates this concept. "Man may have meant it for bad, but God meant it for good." In other words, it's all in divine order.

Think about it. If you believe in God, and if you believe God loves you, then why would a loving God place us on earth to just suffer? The Creator *has* a master plan.

We have now arrived at the third and final point. The notion that we attract negative to us in order to discover who we are, puts a different light on the situation. Our nature in the physical world is good and evil. We attract good. And we attract evil. But in reality we never lose any thing, because we have always had it all. A loved one does not die. They simply transition to another form, a form you may not have yet learned how to communicate with. Your finances can never be lacking, because you have the abundance of the Universe. When you know this in your heart, you see it in your reality.

Our true higher nature is infinitely powerful, wise and loving. We have the inherent power to only attract and create good. However, we must choose to rediscover this power of our own free will. To do this, man must freely choose to die to his will. Man must also choose to learn the ways of love, freedom and righteousness. When we do this, we rediscover that the world of duality is an illusion, upon awakening to this illusion, we return to wholeness with a deeper, richer understanding of who we are. An understanding made possible by our journey though duality.

Now that we clearly understand that we create and attract the negative stressful events in our lives, and these events help us discover and define who we are, we must change our language and thinking about negative events. No event is negative. Stressful events are simply SOS signals, beckoning us back home. When we lose our way in fear, anger, envy or lust, the accompanying stressful events of confusion, lack and limitation soon follow as road markers to show us the way back to the path of love. So you see, it is all in divine order after all.

Ok, let's review. Our world around us is a reflection of what is inside of us, and we have the inherent power to only attract and create good. So the obvious question is: What must I do to attract and create uplifting, loving, prosperous events to me? Where do I start?

Taking responsibility for stress is a good start. We must take full responsibility for every event that happens to us; especially energy-contracting events. When we do this, we begin to move down a path of empowerment; a path where Spirit will empower us to live a life free of oppression and worry; a life where love and prosperity are all around us; a life where our consciousness can bear witness to heavenly states of euphoria. The simple small act of taking responsibility is actually a major key in awakening to all that is.

The concept of empowerment through responsibility is clearly understood in many arenas. We can get a better understanding of how this concept works in spirituality by looking at another arena. Let's take a look at the corporate world. Imagine a company losing money, and the chief executive officer says, "it is not my problem, I was a victim." This executive will probably be victimized a second time. He will be fired.

This basic principle of responsibility works much the same in spirituality. You can choose to abdicate responsibility, and like a corporate executive choose to be a victim. Only to find a never ending cycle of victimization creeping into your life. Or you can choose to be responsible for the circumstances in your reality, and become empowered to change them. It is your choice.

The concept of taking responsibility must be made extremely clear so one does not error or falter when it comes to this critical aspect of our spiritual growth. Let us look at another example: If one has an allergy to strawberries, and eats strawberries anyway, they know their actions were responsible for their breakout of hives. It is easy to accept responsibility when we are obviously responsible. The key is to accept responsibility not only for the obvious; but for everything.

If you are unjustly fired from a job, take responsibility for it, and thank kind Spirit for the new opportunities at hand. If you get sick, take responsibility. If your loved one constantly does the same thing over and over again to annoy you, even after you repeatedly ask them to stop, take responsibility and maintain an attitude of gratitude.

The more responsibility you take, the more you can receive. Ultimately, you must take responsibility for every unevolved act of mankind. Your mortal mind cannot do this, but the mind of your Higher Self, the Christ consciousness, can. The balance comes when you take responsibility for all things, you also sit in heavenly places to receive all things. Just as the chief executive officer sits in a seat to take responsibility for the entire corporation, he receives all accolades for the corporation's success.

Taking responsibility dose not mean you get up out of bed and try to fix everything at once. This would be foolish and frustrating. Taking responsibility often means to acknowledge you are still awakening. Your less desirable circumstances are barometers telling you where you are on the path of awakening, and in what areas spiritual cleansing is necessary.

To perfect taking responsibility for potentially stressful events, adhere to the following:

First: Choose not to become stressed. Quietly observe how you react. You may use the alarm-trigger technique or other methods.

Second: Simply observe the situation, realizing deep within your spirit-heart you have attracted or created it. Feel a resolve to be loving, kind and forgiving to self and others involved.

Third: Take responsibility for it, own it, and then release it. Do not worry about it. Do not let it burden you. Do not beat your self up. Do not wallow in guilt.

It is critical that you not react from guilt. Do not believe you ust feel guilty and blame or condemn yourself to change. This is not ue. To change, you simply need to know and be submissive to Spirit. fact, remove the word guilt from your vocabulary all together. eplace it with the word responsible.

Feeling guilty and beating up on yourself are just other ways avoid responsibility. It is a choice to be stressed. When one 1ooses to feel guilt, they send a clear message to the Universe. They e saying, "I want to stay in misery."

This is how it works. When you worry, beat up on yourself, feel guilty, you are holding on to the energy of the event. Holding 1 can take the form of emotional stress or rerunning the event over 1d over in your mind. Remember, you attract what you think about. ou must release the energy of the event, for when you release this 1ergy, you no longer exude a fragrance that will attract this event to 3u.

To help you release the energy of the event or situation, member you are not yet perfect. The mind of a man is still in 3ntrol, and not the mind of our true Higher Self. When the mind of 1an is still in the driver's seat, you will engage in self defeating words, appropriate attitudes and emotions. So, when you fall short of the 1ark of perfection, simply observe, learn any lesson, atone for that 1ergy, resolve not to go there again, and thank kind Spirit within and ithout for the experience. Then choose to release it and move on to 1e next moment of peace and tranquility. To perfect this will take bedience, courage, practice, intense prayer and meditation, and 2eking the Creator first in all things. Accomplishing this simple rinciple is truly a statement of divine perfection.

Until divine perfection is reached, you may not always nderstand why you are taking responsibility for a thing. It may not 2 for you to understand what an event meant, or what you are to do 30ut it. It may just be for you to experience, and choose how you will react to it. Remember, you are here in the physical plane t experience and remember. Sometimes years pass before Spirit reveal what a particular situation meant.

Upon taking responsibility, you may sometimes wish to as Spirit, your ancestors or spirit guides questions about the even Asking questions is not always necessary or appropriate. Whe appropriate, the following questions may be good to ask. What is i me that attracted this? Is there something I might learn about mysel or change within myself?

The answers to these questions may sometimes be obviou For example, if you have a temper, and it seems like people are alway attacking you, you have attracted their anger. Everyone knows yo are easy to anger. So when they come into your presence their guard are up. They are ready to get caustic to defend themselves from you wrath. Again, we see the principle, you attract whatever you radiat The world around you is a perfect mirror of who and what you choos to be.

Look at your world, your experiences, your relationships, an you will see who you have chosen to be. This way of looking at you world should become so much a part of your thinking, that this is ho you approach every-day life. This is truly taking responsibility.

The concept of the world being a mirror of what is withi sparked an interesting statement and question by one of my student She stated "My husband has been unfaithful. Does this mean I hav the spirit of unfaithfulness in me?" The answer was "no." If she ha this spirit she may have chosen to be unfaithful in response to he husband's actions. Her mirror was showing her the spirit of envy, no infidelity. The mirror's reflection is often indirect. Her life situatio created for her the perfect circumstance to allow this jealous spirit t fully express itself. As it came forth, she could see this unevolve essence within her. She then had the opportunity to acknowledge i thereby, taking responsibility for it, and releasing it. Remember, you piritual journey is not about changing others, but it is about changing elf. As she is open to be cleansed, she will be able to hear clearly rom Spirit how to handle her marriage situation.

Emotions and feelings that cause stress such as fear, anger, jalousy, depression and so forth must be dealt with differently than houghts. One may simply change recurring thought patterns by hoosing to do so, and exerting some discipline. However, in dealing with emotions, courage may be required to face them head on, own p to them, and embrace them. Emotions and feelings must often be xperienced and then released.

To understand how emotions work, let's take a look at this xample. There was a lady who was deathly afraid of spiders. She ould not even look at a picture of a spider without jumping out of her kin. In counseling, under a controlled environment, she was given he opportunity to face her fear. At first she was shown black and white abstract pictures of spiders. As she became comfortable holding nd examining these pictures, she graduated to real, life-like color ictures. After becoming adjusted, she learned how to look through window while she was in another room, at a spider in a glass ontainer. In time and in stages, she entered the room, and held the arantula in her hands.

After the spider lady owned up to her emotions, and faced hem head on, releasing the fear was automatic. The act of facing, mbracing and experiencing an emotion like fear, is often all that is eeded to release it. The key is to own up to the emotion and take esponsibility for it. This does not always happen. A typical example f someone not owning up to their emotions can be seen in an rgument when someone asks, "why are you getting mad?" And your esponse is, "I am not mad!" Have you ever done this? If you find ourself denying you are having a particular emotion, then you robably are having it. So take responsibility for it.

To awaken spiritually, the idea is not only to face the deep seated emotions, but also your every-day feelings. Feelings are fueled by thoughts. Psychological studies suggest humans have thousands of thoughts per day, and 90% of those thoughts are the same thoughts a person had the day before. A person thinks the same thoughts, and feels the same old way day after day. This creates a vicious three part cycle of thoughts, reaction and results. Your thoughts determine your reactions. Your reactions determine your results. Your results determine your thoughts. This cycle is important and requires further explanation.

The first part of the cycle is thoughts and beliefs. What you believe and think determines how you feel, what you do, and how you react. How you react and what you do determines the results you get. The results you get help formulate your beliefs and thoughts about life. Your beliefs and thoughts about life determine how you feel. As this cycle repeats itself, it can negatively reinforce itself. Let's look at an example. As a child, you prayed for a thing, and did not get it. The strong feeling of disappointment set up the belief prayers do not work. So as an adult if you pray for a thing and don't get it, the childhood thoughts are reinforced. Continuous reinforcement of these beliefs intensifies powerless feelings about prayer, and causes a downward spiraling of one's manifesting potential.

This thought-reaction-result cycle emanates from your past experiences. If you continue to react and feel based on your past experiences, you will be destined to remain unevolved. You will spin around and around in the same turmoil of every day existence: never to feel real love; never to know peace; never to experience boundless abundance; never to remember who you are.

The way to stop this cycle is to trust, examine and embrace your feelings; own up to them; take responsibility for them. They will show you what undeveloped qualities lie within you.

If you feel confusion, anger, depression, sadness, envy and so on, you must know these are energies which have no place in your being. Do not associate yourself with being these feelings. Do not say "I am angry", or "I am depressed." The 'I am' statement is a declaration of who you are. These energies are not who you are. As you need to characterize them in order to take responsibility, you may say something like the following. "An energy of anger is in me now." Or "a depressed feeling has come over me in this moment, but I know in Spirit this shall pass. It always does." It is important that when you acknowledge an unevolved energy, you only acknowledge it as being in this present moment. Do not acknowledge it as being your continuous state of being. Avoid saying, "a feeling of depression has come over me" period. This statement says to the Universe you are feeling depression indefinitely. Depression in the moment is a small thing, depression indefinitely is more difficult to overcome.

Another way to stop the cycle of thought, reaction and results is not to react. When you are reacting, you are doing something stemming from a preexisting thought pattern. Instead of reacting, act out of a new you that is being created. As an unevolved feeling comes forth, stop. Examine what is happening. Then choose not to react the same old way. If someone disrespects you, and you feel an energy of anguish coming forth, stop. Do not react with a flippant answer. Instead, choose to send a word or thought of love to yourself and that person. As you practice this consistently, it will interrupt your old downward cycle, give you new feelings and results, and start an upward spiraling cycle toward the light.

The sense of feeling is one of the most underrated but powerful gifts of life. What you are feeling is direct enlightenment as to what is happening within. Your feelings do not lie to you like your thoughts often do. If you are feeling joyful, at that moment, you are bathing in the spirit of joy. If you are feeling anger, the red fiery spirit of anger has engulfed you. Therefore, by examining your feeling, you will get a glimpse of the spiritual energy that has saturated your being in that moment.

Feelings can emanate from several sources other than thoughts and beliefs. They may emanate from your soul. Some African traditions teach feeling pain is the soul crying out for growth. Pain is literally an SOS for the soul.

Other feelings come from Spirit. Have you ever sensed a feeling of love that came from no where in particular? A kind of presence that seemed to engulf you but emanates from you; a warm comforting feeling which was beyond description. Or, have you ever felt a peace fall upon you so profound that it surpassed reason? A peace which lets you realize the every-day world of your life is in utter chaos. These feelings come from Spirit. They are leading you to the grandest experiences one can ever have: Living in the constant presence of the Most High Spirit that dwells within. If you have not sensed these profound life changing feelings, hold on, because as you become "serious" about Spirit these and many more will come. Be patient: it may take years for some.

The most important principle of this chapter is now ready to be introduced. This point is so important if we could have made bells and whistles go off when you opened this page, it would have been done.

The principle is simply this. Your unassisted lower nature is incapable of raising itself. Through the actions of the Higher nature the soul is raised. This unconditional help the Higher nature renders to the lower nature is in response to the lower nature's aspiration for growth. As you sow seeds of love, life and righteousness, cultivate and water them, you will reap love a hundredfold, life everlasting and divine perfection, because Spirit has given you the increase from the beginning of time.

There is simply not enough time for you of your own will and determination, to deal with every stressful issue, contracting emotion

110

or inappropriate thought pattern in your life. The best way to deal with issues in life is to surrender to Spirit, and Spirit will increase your vibrations to be able to sit in heavenly places where unconditional help is always available.

This is what you can do. First, only spend energy dealing with issues or stressful emotions which are so intense they clearly interfere with your natural spiritual growth process. Deal with only one at a time. Then, spend the vast majority of your energy in making passionate prayer, sincere mediation and heart felt spiritual ritual a way of life. In your prayers, meditation and ritual place the Most High Spirit first. As you do this, your vibration in Spirit will increase. As Spirit increases you, dealing with stressful emotions will become easier and faster. Additionally, many of the dark forces that are in you will not be able to stay in this evolving light. You may actually find emotions of fear, anger or hate may just leave you without any work on your part. A proverbial blessing from God.

OK, the dark forces within may be illuminated by having our spiritual vibration increased. But what about dark forces without that come to attack us in the form of spiritual warfare?

Spiritual warfare can truly be a stressful situation if you allow it to be. So do not allow it to be. Do not address spiritual warfare by feeling you must always do battle without. The greatest battleground is within, not in someone else's back yard. The real warfare is in changing the things you can change within you. If you cleanse the heathens and dark forces within you, and you become a beckon of pure Light, no exterior forces can come against you.

Think about this closely. If you accept the Supreme Being, Creator of all, the Universal Consciousness is omnipotent, then what can come against it? Nothing! As more of this Omnipotent potential is awakened in you, it will be harder for any thing to come against you. If you choose to fight spiritual warfare without, you may win a battle here and there, and you may lose a battle here and there. But if you chose to fight the ultimate war within, cleansing your being of all darkness, you will never lose a battle. This is because every battle fought within brings you closer to the Light.

There are techniques you can use to fight the spiritual warfare within, and defeat one of your biggest enemies: stress. The techniques are to live in the present, divorce yourself from outcomes, reduce expectations, perfect acceptance, stop judging and forgive. Each of these points is very important and require detailed examination. Let's begin with living in the present.

Living in the present is another way to reduce stress and grow spiritually. Simply put, you are too busy in the moment to worry about the past or future.

To live effectively in the present requires you always keep foremost in your consciousness that everything is in divine order. If you choose to accept this truth in your heart, it will be easy for you to choose in each and every moment peace, tranquility and love. Right now is the most important time in your life. Fully live in the eternal now, for it is the only moment you really have.

This concept of living in the present has been taught over and over again in spiritual communities. But most people really don't get it. Let's see if it can be made clear in the context of love and joy. Imagine being engaged in something you truly love doing. A hobby, or a passionate conversation with a new and exciting friend. The time simply seems to fly by. That is because you are in the moment, being who you are; without airs; without pretense; without concerns of what will happen. But just enjoying the fullness of the event or conversation.

To be in the present with love and joy is bliss. To be in the present with the absolute unconditional love of Spirit is bliss beyond description.

So the question is, how do I learn to start living in the present? Start by examining your thoughts and deeds, and choose, right now

112

thoughts of love, joy, gratitude, and acceptance. Choose to enjoy life. Don't always be so serious. Take it one moment at a time. As you master your current present moment, you are successful. As you can be positive in this moment, you have won the prize. Upon releasing anger, depression or sadness in this very moment, you are closer to Spirit.

Obviously, one moment leads to the next, and the next, and to eternity. In due season you will experience stopping time in the eternal now.

As you live in the present you must be relentless in your pursuit of Spirit within, steadfast in your passion to know spirit, and honest in your desire to love Spirit with all your heart.

Divorcing yourself from outcomes is a way to live in the present and not become overly concerned with what will happen in the future. You must therefore divorce yourself from outcomes. People's initial response to this statement is usually. "Do you mean, are you saying, I should not have any goals?" No, this is not what we are saying. We are saying that achieving the goal is not the objective. The objective is the process by which the goal is obtained. The process is each and every moment you are engaged in accomplishing the goal.

If the process is the important thing, then you are always successful. If accomplishing the goal is the important thing and the goal is not achieved, you have failed. Failing is stressful. Failing is a false statement to the Universe. Failing declares all things are not in divine order. Failing keeps you from awakening to righteousness. So choose not to fail. Divorce yourself from outcomes. Engage in the process with all your might and strength, and always succeed.

Reducing expectations is something else you can add to the process to prevent stress. If a person expects things to be a certain way, and they are not, this contradiction causes stress. So, if you get stressed because your spouse disappointed you, or a friend violates

113

your expectation, your stress alarm can go off, and your trigger response like "it's all in divine order" will kick in. You may not be able to change the event, but you can change the way you look at it; thereby, stopping stress dead in its tracks.

There is another natural human expectation which causes tremendous stress for many people. This is the desire and need for things to stay the same. Humans are creatures of habit. We do not want things to change. We find security in familiar surroundings. Change is often stressful. On the other hand, evolving spirit beings are always changing. Evolution is change. So embrace change as part of the evolutionary journey.

In one of the Inuit Native American traditions, the spiritual leaders must give away all of their belongings in cycles of seven years. They must not possess anything they owned seven years ago. This is to reinforce the concept of not holding on to the physical, and embracing change.

You do not have to give away all of your belongings. But it would be profitable to develop an attitude which accepts change as a normal and essential part of life. In fact, change is a catalyst for success and growth. So walk in gratitude and humility, giving thanks for being directed to divinity by an ever-changing spiritual journey.

Acceptance and judgement are the next concepts we will deal with to understand how to fight the spiritual warfare within. Acceptance of self is essential. Loving self, not beating up on self, are all acts of self acceptance. These concepts are dealt with in great detail throughout the book. So for purposes of this next discussion, we will look at acceptance of other people's differences, shortcomings and idiosyncracies that directly affect you in relationships.

Relationships can be the most stressful encounters in life. When the spouse starts raging at you, do you choose an encouraging word of love, or an angry response? When the children get on your last nerve, do you act in patience, or do you react in frustration?

114

When people at your job get overbearing, do you choose stress, or peace?

The dichotomy of relationships is they can be stressful, or they can provide the greatest occasions to awaken spiritually. This is because relationships provide non-stop daily challenges for us to see ourselves in our mirror of life, and examine our thoughts, deeds and feelings. Every relationship is a personal gift for growth. It is also a gift you can give to another for their growth. Whether a passing glance from a stranger, or a life long marriage of ups and downs. View all relationships thus, and you will be on the path of awakening.

Acceptance is the key to making relationships work. Acceptance is a stress buster. If someone's behavior is stressing, and out of self-preservation you accept what they are doing, the burden is released.

Acceptance is one of the joys of having a best friend. You can let your guards down, open your heart, and share anything and everything you have done, without the fear of being judged. Your best friend will accept you for who you are, the good and the bad.

Acceptance is actually a quality of the Most High Spirit. Within Universal Consciousness lies all power, but the Universe accepts our choices in life. This is demonstrated in that we have free will. By being tolerant of others, we align ourselves with how Spirit moves.

The key to mastering acceptance is to stop judging. When you engage in seemingly innocent colloquial terms, you are judging. For example: "That was wrong of you." "You should have never done that!" "How could you have done that?" "You ought to be ashamed of yourself."

If you engage in gossiping, you are judging. Think about it. If the gossip is not juicy, it's not gossip. The act of gossiping means you have judged someone's actions to be scandalous, lurid or sexually promiscuous.

115

Everyone has heard you should not judge people, and if you judge people, you will be judged the same way. But how and why does this happen? The next explanation will make clear how judging brings similar judgement and consequences to you.

To judge means to find someone innocent or guilty. To find someone guilty is to say they are the culprit, which is in itself an automatic condemnation. If you think someone's actions are wrong or inappropriate, you have labeled them the culprit, and condemned them in your thoughts. To condemn someone in your thoughts, means you have projected negative energy to them. Thoughts are really spiritual energy forms. Remember, whatever energy, or spiritual fragrance you put out into the Universe, comes back to you.

In judging, your negative thoughts cast toward another is a direct attack on them spiritually. Whenever you attack someone spiritually, you invite spiritual attack on yourself, as well as everyone around you: family, friends and loved ones. Even if you are not conscious that this spiritual warfare is going on, it is. Spiritual laws work regardless of your being conscious of them. Just like physical laws work regardless of your knowledge. Fire will burn you, whether you know it or not.

Living under constant spiritual attack is stressful. It is a world where people are always spreading rumors about you; not being fair to you; victimizing you for no apparent reason. To ease the stress of this world, stop judging others. Stop talking about others, unless it is uplifting. When this has become a way of life for you, your world of victimization, back-biting and injustice will begin to vanish.

For most people, judging has been a way of life. Changing your behavior from judging overnight, may not change your circumstances as quickly. Be patient. Trust Spirit. Believe in the process, and continue to live without judgement. Look for the positive in every person. See the divine light in everyone, even if it is dull. Compliment someone as often as possible. As you identify with

116

the good in people, this is what people will show you. This is what the Universe will give you.

Many people believe you cannot safely navigate through life without judging. They assume you must judge a person or situation to know how to respond. This is a common mistake people make because they do not understand the difference between judgment and discernment.

Discernment means to perceive, comprehend or recognize. Discernment is not concerned with innocence or guilt. Discernment simply recognizes a thing for what it is without judgement or condemnation. The difference between judgement and discernment is that judgement is often based on previous experiences and social norms, whereas true discernment is based on spiritual truth. The following story will make this point clear.

A ragged dressed, dirty and obviously homeless man was standing on a busy highway jumping up and down, waving his arms and throwing sticks at passing cars. People judged his actions to be of a homeless crazy man and kept on driving. Eventually a lady discerned in her heart something was terribly wrong. So she called the highway patrol. An hour later an officer drove by and saw the man in the act. When the officer stopped to arrest him, the homeless man explained a car had gone off the highway and crashed in the woods out of sight. He had been trying to stop someone to get help for hours.

Everyone who passed this man on the highway, except this one lady, judged him by his appearance. Judgement looks on the surface and sees a thing as it appears to be. Discernment looks below the surface and sees a thing like it really is. Judgement is based on man's common sense. Discernment is based on the common sense of Spirit.

Spiritual discernment is not only a valuable asset for every day life, it is a necessity for spiritual enlightenment. Pure spiritual discernment functions best when the energy of judgement does not cloud the air. Know that all people are divine creations of Spirit, and release the need to judge.

If you fall into the trap of judging someone, then remember in thought you have sentenced and condemned them. So you must now forgive them and yourself.

Forgiving is essential to spiritual awakening. You must forgive all transgressions. On a spiritual path you cannot afford to resent, blame or hold a grudge against anyone or anything. If you do, you are condemning yourself.

The Our Father or Lord's Prayer in the Bible has a strange verse that as a child I could never understand: The phrase is "forgive us our debts (trespasses) as we forgive our debtors (trespassers)." Finally, as an adult I understood this phrase is simply a reminder of a spiritual law. What we put out comes back.

To be unforgiving is to blame. Blame is defined as a form of condemnation. For as you choose not to forgive, you hold the dark energy of condemnation, and as you hold this energy within, it condemns you. Additionally, to condemn another in thought is to curse or spiritually attack that person.

Thoughts of blame declare to the Universe you were a victim; victimization disempowers you to do anything about it; this brings on resentment.

Resentment is a driving force for thoughts. Thoughts of resentment nag at your consciousness, erode your peace of mind, and causes stress in the physical body.

To let you see where you are on the scale of forgiveness, let's try an exercise. Read the following poem.

Universe, and all that is, I make a decree.
Forgive me, and set me free.
Let there be no stress in me.
Give me prosperity, and a life of glee.

118

But do this kind Spirit only to a degree.
The degree I can forgive others,
and set them free.

Now say this poem out loud and mean it. Say it several times with as much passion as you can muster before reading further.

If you did not mind saying this poem out loud with passion, then good. You may be on your way to forgiving. The next part of this exercise is to search your consciousness for anyone or anything not forgiven. This includes wars, oppression, discrimination, slavery as well as personal transgressions. Examine yourself for any grudges, hard feelings or bitterness you may have held on to. Do you still feel uneasy about someone who owes you money, or who talked about you, or treated you unfairly, disrespected you, or ignored you? Be as thorough and honest with yourself as possible. Do this before reading on.

Next, imagine every time you say this poem a genie will instantly appear. Upon appearing he will literally rob you of prosperity and joy, and curse you with stress for every unforgiving thought you have.

Now with the genie standing over you, are you willing to again passionately say the poem knowing the genie will read your thoughts of unforgiveness. If you can do this with a clear conscious, you are further along the path of forgiving.

Living in a consciousness of unforgiveness and resentment is like a genie standing over your shoulders. This consciousness robs you of peace and joy. This concept is easy to comprehend if one is obsessed with resentment and seeking revenge. But it must be understood that this concept is also true if you have any dark energy of resentment lingering within you. Dark energy decreases spiritual vibration. You have unknowingly declared spiritual warfare upon yourself. With this internal warfare going on, lasting peace can never be found.

Finding internal peace is one of the most important quests in a person's life. To understand peace, another rendition of the classic age-old tale of wealth, health and peace will be told.

From a young boy, Harry always wanted to be rich. He dreamed about it, talked about it, and even became a master Monopoly player at age seven. By the age of 21 he had earned his first million dollars. By 25 he was a multi-millionaire. However, his fast paced life soon caught up with him. At 27 he was diagnosed with an advanced stage of AIDS.

The fear of death terrified Harry. Making money was no longer important. His obsession in life turned to finding a cure. During the next few years he spent millions traveling around the world following leads on miracle cures, but one by one they each failed. His AIDS was progressing, and at each failed attempt at a cure, the fear of death grew stronger and stronger. Harry's anger at the healers grew deeper and deeper. He needed a cure, and he blamed these people for selling him false hope. He became so upset he spent hundreds of thousands of dollars to expose and discredit these healers as charlatans. As this quest ensued, his wealth diminished and his health plummeted.

As Harry's body wasted away and became riddled with secondary diseases and pain, he dropped his vengeful obsession, and his need to find a cure. He finally faced his fear of death. Upon facing this, Harry realized the most important thing he could do now was to find peace of mind. So he read everything he could get his hands on about peace. This led him to Spirit, prayer and meditation. Then one night around midnight, when Harry was meditating, a sudden realization came over him. The experience was so penetrating he could hardly contain himself. All he could do was cry uncontrollably. He was crying tears of joy. He had found peace. He realized in his spirit that death was only an awakening. He was no longer obsessed with anything, nor did he feel the need for anything in life. For the first time he had a deep understanding of freedom, fulfillment, joy and even love. He also realized his earlier obsession with wealth and sex was just a misguided quest to find these things.

Immediately after this night, Harry began living in the present. He gave thanks for each new day he lived, and enjoyed that day to the max. Then Harry's health started to improve. His immune system strengthened and he gained weight. His bankrupted financial empire exploded with new financial gains. Harry lived years longer than it was predicted, and he spent this time helping other AIDS patients find peace.

This fictional story about Harry dramatically depicts the desires of most humans. People want financial security. But if challenged with severe health problems, the need for health supersedes the desire for money. Money, then, simply becomes a tool to obtain health, and if health can't be obtained, then the need for peace of mind is the most important quest in life. Unfortunately, in this society our priorities are backwards. Life would be a much better journey if people only realized finding peace of mind is more important than finding wealth, job security, or the acquisition of any physical "stuff." Contrary to popular belief, you can not find peace and freedom with money.

Harry had to learn this lesson the hard way. What Harry learned was the same principles discussed in the latter part of this chapter. Let's see how.

When Harry faced his terrifying fear of death, and forgave and released those who had robbed him of his wealth, he was able to accept his life's situation and take responsibility for it. In doing so Harry understood he must find peace. The pursuit of inner peace led him to Spirit. To find the Spirit of peace, Harry became immersed in prayer and meditation. Meditation is like a doorway leading to inner

121

peace. If you traverse this doorway long enough with passion and sincerity, the fragrance of peace will permeate your spirit.

When the Spirit of peace fell upon Harry, he was no longer concerned about the final outcome of his physical life, which was death. He accepted physical death without judging and expecting it to be the final episode of life. This gave him the freedom to move on with his life. Harry began living in the present which revitalized his wealth, and allowed him to find fulfilling work with other AIDS patients.

The stress of immediate foreseen physical death is one of the greatest stresses most can imagine. However, thousands of people every year come to terms with this ultimate stress. If this can be accomplished, then surely you can overcome the less dramatic stresses of your life, and find internal peace.

Choose not to be like Harry and have to face death before you seek to find peace. Choose to reap the fruits of Spirit which are joy, love, and peace, while you still have years of life left. Choose not to live a life of fear, but a life of peace. For fear is the number one enemy of peace.

Finding peace requires clearly understanding its relationship to fear and need. First, need is an energy that is like unto lust. Lust is the ultimate irrational need taken to extremes. It can drive one to destruction. True lasting inner peace and freedom can never be obtained when you are held prisoner by lusting for anything: sex, money, material goods or friendship. Most people clearly understand the destructive energy of lust, but most overlook at its destructive cousin called need.

If you need a thing, then the door to fear is opened: fear that you might not get what is needed, or lose what is needed. For example, if you need someone's approval to have peace of mind, you may fear that person might not give their approval. If the person does not give you their approval or kindness, you might get angry. If the

122

person persists at disapproving you, and being unkind to you, you may eventually dislike them. If dislike becomes strong enough, it turns into hate. If you hate someone, you will stay angry with them, and be apprehensive - a form of fear - about further encounters with the person. If the problem persists with intensity long enough, frustration or depression may set in. In addition to all of this, fear will cause you to act aggressively toward another out of perceived self defense.

Fear is the seed energy which creates anger, hatred, depression, jealousy and so forth. Expression of these emotional energies also prevents internal peace. Let's look at other examples.

If you need someone to be faithful to you, and you fear they are not, then your peace may be robbed by jealousy. If your need to eat, pay the rent, and acquire certain physical things is the only reason you work at a particular job or career, then you are obviously working out of a need for things. Fear of not acquiring the things you need is the only reason you continue to work this stressful job. This fear based, everyday life experience turns into stress, depression, resentment, anger and so forth. In fact, more heart attacks are reported at 9:00 a.m. Monday morning than any other time. After a beautiful weekend of freedom and rest, the stress of needing to go back to work causes heart attacks.

With unshakable internal peace, no exterior circumstances or persons can alter your state of mind. When Harry found peace he no longer needed anything in life. He found freedom, fulfillment, joy and love. Just like Harry, when you find peace of mind, you will also need nothing to find freedom, fulfillment, and joy. There is a bonus. Just as Harry found new financial growth and meaningful work with other AIDS patients, you will also discover newly found success in your career and personal life. With peace of mind, life flows easier, work is more productive, and loving relationships happen effortlessly. To make this point clear, the following examples are given.

With the peace of Spirit, you will have such a great sense of self worth that you will need nothing from others. Others will be drawn to you, and they will like, respect and honor you because they see something different, noble and royal about you. This is why spiritual masters have followings even if they do nothing to attract them.

With the peace of Spirit, you will have the clarity to find, be led to, or create a new career if the old one is not to your liking. Peace brings internal clarity. Internal clarity allows one to hear Spirit. When one hears Spirit, and is obedient, one will be led to a more prosperous life. This prosperity may manifest by finding work that you do not out of need, but out of the joy. Upon this happening, your work is no longer need based and stressful, but joy-based and fulfilling. I have witnessed this on numerous occasions.

The need, fear and peace equation is simple. Need = fear - peace: Need means (equals) having fear without (minus) peace. In other words if you do not need a thing, you will not fear losing it, or not having it. Thus, if you do not need anything, you do not fear anything. If you do not fear anything, the other secondary emotions of fear do not show up in your life. Without these emotions, internal peace is easy to find.

The inverse to this equation is also true. When you have the unshakable internal peace of Spirit, you do not need anything to find fulfillment, comfort or security in life. The principle here is you do not 'need' anything. You may desire or envision having everything, but this is not a need. Desire is merely a preference. Preferences do not open the door to fear like need does. If you prefer a thing, and it does not show up, then so be it.

To find peace: Cultivate a need for nothing. Envision manifesting everything. Be open to receive it all. Give joyful thanks for whatever appears.

Ultimately unshakable internal peace comes from being in Spirit. So as it has been stated over and over again, put Spirit first, and be committed to your spiritual evolution. Maintain a life of prayer, meditation and ritual. This keeps you in the presence of Spirit, and Spirit's nature is peace.

Additionally, internal peace comes by knowing 'it is all in divine order'. Repeat this affirmation over and over again, especially when you feel something has gone wrong. Eventually your subconscious will get the message. For some, it happens instantly; for others, years. Be patient.

One final note for this chapter. Do not set your ideals on transforming stress into success so high that your ideals become a source of stress. Remember you are still awakening into perfection. Until you are perfect, there will be a need for frequent self nurturing and habitual self acceptance. Read this chapter over and over again, until the concepts and ideas become part of you. As this is done, the Suffering-Oppression-Sorrow will Save-Our-Souls.

Thank you kind Spirit.

Common Sense Exercise: Lessen the Impact of Stress

There are many ways to lessen the impact of stress on your body, mind and spirit. Lessening the impact does not stop the source of stress, but it can halt dis-ease and dis-harmony. Physical exercise, stretching, yoga, breathing exercises, and massage therapy are all effective ways to reduce the impact of stress.

Get involved with a physical routine you can maintain. Consistency is the secret to success with exercise. Park you car a

125

good walking distance from work. This will cause you to consistently get exercise by walking each day. Learn several simple yoga or stretching exercises that only take five to ten minutes. Then do them routinely before you get dressed each morning.

Practice this simple breathing exercise two to three times a day. Breath in deeply though the nose, extending the abdomen for a count of four. Hold it seven seconds. Then breath out of your mouth, with the tip of your tongue on the roof of your mouth, for a count of eight. Repeat this cycle eight times. This breathing exercise only takes several minutes to do, but if done consistently it will have an effect on your biological age and peace of mind.

If you choose to get massages, set up a regular schedule. For example, schedule with the therapist every first and third Tuesday of each month. By establishing a routine, it will be easier to keep it up consistently.

Additional ways to reduce the effect of stress are to listen to relaxing music, sit in a sauna, Jacuzzi or whirlpool, or take a hot bath infused with herbs, such as chamomile, valerian, rosemary or lime blossoms. Aroma therapy with essential oils like lavender is extremely soothing.

Meditating is the most important technique for lessening the impact of stress. It relaxes the body, reverses the stress response, and decreases the biological age. Meditation also exposes the source of stress.

Thank you kind Spirit.

Chapter 5

Supernatural Events & Spiritual Healing

How to make spiritual events part of your every day life.

We had no agenda other than uplifting Spirit. Our retreat group was in fervent prayer, passionate ritual and being moved by Spirit. One lady was unctioned to step into the frigid waters of the stream, and spiritually cleanse herself with the healing waters of Mother Earth. Spirit was flowing through her as if it were the last days on earth. She pull each of us, one by one into the waters. As we continued dancing to the rhythm of Spirit in our hearts, we felt the very pulse of the Native American spirits that once inhabited this sacred cavern.

As we left the sacred cave in amazement, one of the ladies with us slipped on the lose gravel. She badly sprained her ankle. By the time we sat down at a table, she was riddled in pain, her ankle had swollen, and she could hardly walk. As I sat at the table with her, watching her in obvious pain, I became more and more bewildered as to why she had not asked for a healing. Especially, in light of the fact she knew healing energy flows through me, and Spirit was so high in this place. We had all just witnessed awesome events. There was no question in my mind that she could be completely healed in moments. I thought she must surely know this. In fact, she had personally witnessed healings that I had done. So I wondered, "why won't she ask?"

127

I did not volunteer my services as a vehicle for spiritual healing. I was following the teaching of my former Native American spiritual mentor. He wisely taught that one is not to heal, unless the one in need of healing asks, or the Great Spirit tells you to.

As I watched her almost in tears, it became too much for me to keep my mouth shut. I said, "you know! I'm a healer." Then after coaxing her, she finally said, "I did not want to be a bother, but if you get time, you can pray for me." My wife and I did pray for her. By the next day, she was vigorously dancing to the drums in high heel sandals, with no pain.

This story is a typical example of many just like it. I have seen many situations in which people would not ask for a healing, and were in the presence of a spiritual healer. I have often asked "why?" The response was usually the same: "I just did not think about it", "I forgot"; or, "I did not want to be a bother."

If these individuals thought they would really be healed, they would not forget, or think a healer to be busy. They don't forget to go to the doctor. In their hearts, these individuals do not believe they could be healed spiritually. So they do not seriously consider spiritual healing as a viable option.

This brings us to the first reason why more spiritual supernatural events do not happen on a regular basis in people's lives. People simply do not ask, or seriously look for it.

So it would seem logical to assume that once a person had experienced a supernatural event like spiritual healing, they would remain open to seek it. Well, let's go back to the lady with the twisted ankle. You would think she would not make the same mistake of not asking again. She personally had been healed. She personally knows how Spirit can stop pain. Well, she did. She made the same mistake again.

A month after the retreat, her dearly loved three year old child needed an operation. Again, I had to volunteer to pray for her son, after the operation. Again, why had she not looked for a spiritual healing?

Why people do not look for supernatural events more in their lives is even more perplexing when you examine the written evidence for spiritual events. There are thousands of documented spiritual healings, as well as documented facts published in scientifically monitored journals about the existence of paranormal events. However, all of this published information goes right over the heads of people. This is why the lady did not ask for a healing for her son, it went right over her head.

To explain this concept, several examples must be examined. We can clearly understand that intellectual information can go over someone's head. If a Ph.D. in mathematics tries to explain to a high school student the power of his latest math theorem, the student would hear, but would not really understand. The math would obviously go right over the student's head.

What we must realize is, beliefs are similar to the intellect. Things can go right over someone's intellect or belief system. For instance, a spiritual healer can tell a person all about the supernatural miracles she has experienced. The person would hear the stories, but would not be able to accept them, or incorporate them into their every- day reality. The information would go right over the person's belief system. You can no more cram information into your intellect, than you can cram information into your belief system.

Several years after I had learned how to be a vehicle for healing energy to flow though me, I was still surprised each time I witnessed a person being healed. Even though I could feel the energy flowing, it was hard for me to believe people were getting well just because I put my hands on them.

Now we are really ready to bring home this concept that spiritual events, and the spiritual life, goes right over people's heads. This will be done with a riddle.

129

A man and his son had a terrible car accident. The father was killed. They rushed the son to the hospital, and the surgeon came in, and looked at the boy, and said "Oh, I can't operate on this boy -- he's my son." Now, who was the surgeon? I heard this riddle on television years ago, and I have told it dozens of times in workshops around the country to large groups of people. It never fails that the vast majority of people do not know the answer. If the answer to the riddle is not immediately apparent to you, I suggest that you stop reading for a moment and see if you can figure it out.

Many people will answer this riddle by saying that the surgeon is the stepfather, or godfather or even heavenly Father. But of course this is not correct. If you have not yet figured this riddle out, are you a sexist? In other words, do you discriminate against women, whether you are a man or a women?

Another hint for the riddle. If we change the riddle to a nurse came in, and said "I can't help operate on this boy because he's my son." Who's the nurse? His mother of course. Interestingly enough, the vast majority of logical people, and women's rights activists, can not figure out the surgeon must be the mother.

This is only a riddle because in your heart you believe that only men are surgeons. Your thinking is controlled by your heart or subconscious programing. You know better in your head, but not your heart.

Psychologists say that 80% of a person's programming occurs before age six. Small children are programmed to think of men in certain roles, and women in certain other roles. Even though a person has grown up, and seen female doctors, one's childhood programing would not let them figure out this riddle. The same situation occurs with supernatural events. Even though a person's logical mind will say that supernatural events occur, when confronted with one it is dismissed, or explained away as a coincidence. This is done time and time again, because we have been programmed not to believe supernatural events.

How often has a child been told to grow up, and stop playing with their imaginary friends. Since we have been programmed not to believe in the supernatural, our beliefs set up self-fulfilling prophecies. We live in a culture lacking an awareness of spirituality.

Even if you consider yourself to be spiritual, you must acknowledge you have been programmed not to believe in the supernatural. That is why I was a healer for years, and still found it amazing each time a person was healed. I recall when this was first brought to may attention. At a spiritual conference, my mentor, a Native American spiritual healer, had healed quite a number of very sick people. One of the conference coordinators came to me and excitedly proclaimed. "I did not expect so many miracles to happen." I responded in great curiosity, "what miracles?" She then started to tell me of all the people my mentor had healed. I patiently waited for her to finish talking, because I thought she was just rambling. When she finished telling me of the spiritual healing, I asked again with excitement. "What miracles, tell me about the miracles?" She looked at me with a puzzled look on her face and said, "the spiritual healings are the miracles." When I told my mentor this story. He said, "good you are finally accepting spiritual healings as part of the natural, and not the supernatural." You are becoming a healer.

Even though a person can read books about supernatural spiritual events, and experience a few of them, they will not really believe enough in their heart to totally embrace and trust spirituality as the principal way of life. They have not received enough of the feminine receptive spirit of faith, to create their reality supernaturally. It requires seeing miracles continuously, experiencing the flow of spiritual energy, and increasing one's vibratory energy frequency. It requires making prayer and meditation a way of life, and changing the fundamental belief that you are a physical being. We are spiritual beings, just having a physical experience.

The key to having more supernatural events happen in your life is to believe it is so. Have faith in the omnipotent nature of Spirit within.

A practical way to start implementing this goal immediately is to examine your thoughts and deeds. Psychologists say 80% of the time you do not know why you do what you do. You are on auto pilot, functioning out of subconscious programming - most of which was placed there before age six. This process causes you to automatically, without thought, reject any supernatural event that is occurring right before your eyes.

Look for supernatural events every day of your life. The more you look for coincidences, signs, wonders and supernational events, the more you will find them. The more you find them, the more you will begin to believe them. The more you believe them, the greater your faith becomes. Increased faith attracts more supernatural events, so you will experience more, and greater events as you look for them.

It is important to recognize even the little miracles in life like: When someone offers you something to drink when you are thirsty: When you are running late, and you find a parking space right up front. When you wake up with a headache, but when time came for the important meeting, it was gone. These little events are all blessings from Spirit within and without, and you created them. Start seeing it so, and you will start opening up yourself to a greater presence in Spirit.

Avoid the trap of dismissing unusual events as coincidences. There are no coincidences in life. There is a divine order. As you realize this, you will be open more to synchronicity. Synchronicity is the coming together of unusual circumstances, which many dismiss as coincidences.

For each supernatural event, blessing, lesson or good tiding you experience, immediately give thanks to Spirit. By acknowledging a higher source for the things in your life, you will begin to awaken to the realization of being one with this Source.

The take-home message is, if you recognize Spirit in all that you do, your faith will be increased. With increased faith, supernatural events will become a way of life.

Faith is one of the most important requirements for supernatural events and spiritual healings. However, so much misinformation has been given about faith that it is one of the most misunderstood principles in spirituality. It need not be. The concept of faith is very simple. Faith is an energy that draws things to you. This magnetic energy of faith is so extremely important it will be explained in several different ways.

The simplest definition of faith is one of the oldest: "Faith is the substance of things hoped for; the evidence of things not seen." This Bible definition of faith says a lot. Faith is a substance. It is an actual energy substance. Its nature is like a magnet that attracts desires and hopes.

Think of a magnet. A magnet has a positive charge and a negative charge. The two opposite charges attract each other. Different spiritual energies have characteristics like positive and negative. For example, if you want to attract and hold a positive energy form, like healing energy, you need a negatively charged energy form like faith to pull in the healing energy, and hold it.

With this concept in mind, let's examine it in more detail. So faith is a negatively charged energy; energies for healing, manifestation, and miracles are positively charged. The negative energy of faith attracts and holds the positive energies of healing and manifesting. So if you have enough faith, you can literally be like a vacuum cleaner sucking up every healing, manifesting, miracle energy in the universe.

Hold this example, and look at faith using another paradigm. Ancient scriptures imply that faith is feminine. To create, one needs the union of the feminine and masculine energy. The masculine energy puts forth the seed, and the feminine energy receives the seed, and births it. Faith receives the spiritual seed of healing, and births it.

Now let's look at it another way. It has been discussed in great detail in this book that thoughts are masculine energy forms. The masculine, positively charged thought form goes out into the universe to impregnate 'things' for creation. They are like seeds that need to fall on fertile ground to grow. Faith, of course, is a feminine energy. Like fertile ground, it can receive the positive masculine energy thought forms, and birth them into creation. Thus, to manifest, heal or otherwise create, you need the masculine thought to impregnate, and the feminine energy of faith to birth.

So when you pray for a thing or an event, you put out into the universe a masculine seed to be amplified by the Source within and without. Amplification can occur by orchestrating synchronized events. To receive the event prayed for, which is symbolically the amplified seed, and is literally the synchronized event, you must have enough faith to pull it back to you, hold it, and birth it. This is the secret of prayer and faith. This is the key to experiencing supernatural events.

Metaphorically, Faith is a divine celestial feminine being, with a womb capable of birthing stars. Her feminine beauty calls out, and attracts the heavenly Father with seeds to birth the universe.

Faith was conceived by Mother Wisdom, impregnated with Divine Will, and brought forth of oneness. Faith's palace is the heart of every human being.

Let's examine this a bit more, and look at an example of spiritual healing. Spiritual healing works through a spiritual healer because the healer takes the posture of the masculine, and conducts positively charged healing energy. The healing energy actually radiates over the patient, which causes a change in the molecular composition of the patient. If the healer can radiate enough positively charged healing energy, the patient will be healed. However, if the patient can take a feminine posture, and radiate negatively charged faith energy, the positively charged healing energy will stick, and the healing will work more. If the patient has no faith, and cannot hold the healing energy, it makes the healer's job harder. The healer has to conduct more healing energy for the healing to work.

Now that faith is demystified, it becomes easy to see why faith is needed for healing. This is why Jesus often asked people he was about to heal, "do you have faith." Jesus understood if the person had faith his job would be easier.

It's like this: Imagine a person having extremely bad diarrhea because of a bacterial infection. Everything the person takes runs right through in minutes. If the person takes antibiotics to kill the bacteria, the antibiotic passes right through the person, and the bacteria will live. One solution to this problem is large amounts of antibiotics with the hope of some of it being absorbed before most of it is passes through. This may be dangerous, because there may be side effects from large doses of antibiotics.

This example is similar to spiritual healing. The person without faith is like the patient with diarrhea. They cannot hold the spiritual energy, it passes right through them before it has a chance to work. One way to solve the problem is to give the person more spiritual healing energy. However, this could be dangerous because this much intense energy going though a person could have side effects.

I recall an occasion in which one of my spiritual mentors had to stop sending healing energy because the intensity of the energy was too great for the person's body. Specifically, he was healing a fibroid tumor, intense heat had built up, the tumor was being dissolved. However, the woman had little faith. In his desire to finish the healing, he started pushing his own energy. Then Spirit told him to stop, because his energy was starting to destroy tissue rather than the tumor.

If we look at the example of the diarrhetic patient further, there is something else that can be done instead of administering more antibiotic. Simply treat the person with a medicine that will slow down the diarrhea first, then give the healing antibiotic. As you stop the person from passing everything that goes into them, they will be able to hold the antibiotic long enough for it to kill the diarrhea causing bacteria.

The same is true with spiritual healing. To stop the healing energy from passing right through a person, simple treat for a lack of faith. This is why Jesus asked, "do you have faith." He was treating the person for spiritual diarrhea before he administered the spiritual antibiotic that destroys the source of the illness.

With this background, another concept of spiritual healing can be understood. If a spiritual healer works on a person, and the person receives temporary relief, and the illness returns. Several things could have happened. First and obviously, the healing may have been incomplete. The healing energy emanating from the healer may not have been adequate to cause sufficient molecular changes.

Second, the person may not have believed the healing would last. Belief is a form of negatively charged energy. So in the state of unbelief, the person could not hold the positively charged healing energy received. Additionally, this disbelief attracts fear, doubt, and worry, which are thought forms that bit-by-bit, moment -by-moment, shift the healed matter back to is original diseased state.

On the other hand, if a person believes in their heart, or has faith, the healing was complete, then a different series of events happens. This faith holds the healing energy like glue, and the damaged tissue is constantly assaulted. In time, the healing is complete.

This seemingly theoretical description of holding healing energy has merit. It is common knowledge among many spiritual healers that a person who feels the heat or presence of the healing energy long after the healer has stopped, often gets healed. It is believed these people feel this energy for prolonged periods of time because of faith. However, there are other factors not discussed here.

Please understand that each and every person has the ability to heal themselves. Each person has the ability to receive positive healing energy from Source within and without. Everyone also has the ability to hold this energy with faith.

If you have been on a spiritual path for years, and you have a problem healing yourself, then examine yourself. Here are questions you might consider. Is it an inability to shut down your mind, and let the healing energies flow? Is it a lack of faith? Understand this, a lack of faith can manifest indirectly through need. This has been outlined before. If you have a strong need to be healed, this may result in subtle fear you might not be healed. Fear can manifest as doubt. Doubt is the opposite of faith. One further thing to consider is self sabotaging thoughts, like being unworthy?

Whatever the case, understand that the ultimate answer and solution can come from Spirit within. Do not lust after an answer. Seek earnestly, and release it. The answer will come at the correct time, in the correct season.

Now let's return to faith. The key is to have faith, and not so much belief. For the purpose of this guide book, faith is not the same thing as belief. Belief is like the little sister of faith. Looking at it another way, faith is belief, but belief is not always faith.

Belief can stem from the mind of man. One can believe something that is not true, or one can believe a thing that is destructive. Thus, with belief, one can attract to themselves masculine energy that comes from the destructive ego-driven will of man. One

137

can attract fear, anger, hatred, depression, jealousy, worry, and so forth, if one buys into the belief system of the world of duality.

Belief is a powerful energy. It can birth wondrous things, but its power is limited because it does not come from oneness.

For the purpose of this text, faith is a higher energy form. Faith has it origin in oneness. All things are possible with faith. Faith attracts higher divine energy. Faith is discriminating. She will not awaken in hearts that are void of wisdom, love and purity.

So the question is how to acquire faith. One way is to step out on faith. The more you step forward in faith, the more your conscience will accept the process. The more your consciousness accepts the process, the more success you will have. As you see success, the old beliefs will be invalidated, and new beliefs in spiritual healing will increase.

There are numerous other things that can be done. Here are a few basic ingredients: working with your belief system; making prayer, and the feminine act of meditation a way of life; being positive; placing Spirit first; being obedient to the unctions of Spirit within; living a life of gratitude; and on, and on, and on.

Faith is part of a holistic spiritual package. As your vibratory energy frequency increases in a balanced way, the energy of faith is there with you. Remember, unlimited, universal faith is already in you. It was placed in your heart from the beginning of time.

The quest is not so much to find faith, as it is to release it. Releasing faith by tearing down the old belief system that keeps her in bondage. Create new opportunities by positive thought, which gently nudges faith out of her long sleep, revitalizing her in the healing waters of meditation and uplifting her with the spirit of gratitude.

In the remaining portions of this chapter, we will continue to examine the holistic spiritual approach to evolution. This will increase faith, and transform your earth-bound walk into a wondrous journey through supernatural worlds. The holistic journey will continue with being positive.

Being Positive is one of the most elementary but profound ingredients of personal and spiritual success. The consequences of not being positive has been discussed throughout this book. Only one point needs to be re-emphasized. It is important to remind yourself of the positive things you do, as well as the supernatural events that happen to you. This is well understood by one African tradition.

In this African culture when someone does wrong, or does an injustice to another, a serious ritual takes place. The transgressor stands in the middle of a circle with everyone in the village surrounding him. Then everyone, one by one, walks up to the transgressor, points their finger in his face, and avidly reminds him of something good he did. We should learn this lesson not only for ourselves, but for our transgressors as well.

Incorporate this concept into your spiritual life. As you keep a diary, write the supernatural events and spiritual healings that occur. Read them periodically. If you do this for years, you will be totally surprised at how many spiritual things have happened. This will help your faith beyond measure.

This is also important because there is a self sabotaging mind, that will tell you that you have not really grown spiritually over the years. Well, if you have a diary, you can point one-by-one to every supernatural event, and avidly remind that saboteur of your good deeds.

Self sabotage is one spiritual energy you must beware of. Self sabotage is a subtle energy that hits you blind side.

This is how self sabotage works. A victory is about to be gained, but old thought patterns of unworthiness return. Then your subconscious mind goes to work creating events to validate this belief. The validation is seen in the victory being lost. Other common sabotaging beliefs that many people have are: Money is the root of all evil. To accomplish something I must work hard. Time is precious, so I have to rush. Great success brings great problems. I must please others. I must be right. I am not good enough. I am not pretty enough. These sometimes seemingly rational beliefs are insidiously self destructive.

On the spiritual level, you have been programmed to believe that: Your consciousness resides in the mind-body. What you receive spiritually is limited to what you can do, or how much you sacrifice. All prayers are not answered. Manifestation is a hit-and-miss thing. Life ends at death, so you fear death. True and unlimited abundance on all planes is hard to attain. You can't quiet your mind. You are a separate human being. Supernatural events like instantaneous healing are not natural, and so forth, and so on.

Self sabotage might show up as follows. You are about to have a major break through, and you get sick, depressed, tired, angry, or every possible distraction shows up, if you seem to always hit a wall concerning a certain specific thing; if you are led by Spirit to follow through on a dream, and fear kicks in; if you believe it is too good to be true.

Now hear this! If someone says to you, "you brought this on yourself," and you immediately deny it with passion, this is the sign of self sabotage. If you were not sabotaging self, you would not need to express passion. This passion strongly keeps the hidden sabotage belief. To stay hidden is the nature of a saboteur. Self sabotage by definition means you are not aware you are doing it. That is why it is called sabotage. If you knew you were doing it, it would be called foolish. Look for the saboteur to be revealed by an emotional response to a word from a friend or loved one, a casual conversation, TV programming, or even a message from Spirit.

There is an extremely important point that must be made. Some refuse to believe that self sabotage is anything they would ever do. Believe it. If you are alive and breathing, you have done it.

To make the point clear, self sabotage happens on a societal as well an individual basis. In the United States, the land of liberty, freedom and justice for all, women are still paid less than men. Housing discrimination laws are prosecuting more people than ever, and no one wants to take responsibility for it. A supervisor will 'unknowingly' give a woman appointments that are less demanding. Then wonder what happened to her at the end of the year when her productivity is less than the men's. He then gives her a lower raise based on productivity. This happens all the time, and you are not immune to it.

The riddle about the father and son shows us how we have been programmed with certain thoughts, and regardless of our self image, these programs sabotage us. One of the best ways to grow spiritually is to recognize, take responsibility for, and release self sabotage when it shows its ugly face. There is an experiment that you can do.

Self sabotage experiment is what it is called. Start by sitting down with pen in hand. The goal is to write down everything which you think can prevent spiritual growth. Start by categorizing these beliefs in different sections. Use as many sections as needed. Some of the sections could be: What prevents regular meditation? Why don't people pray more? Why is clairvoyance not experienced by more people? Why don't people have more out-of-body experiences? Why do people not dream more, or have lucid dreams? Why can people not trust? What prevents one from having faith? Why don't people love Spirit, or God [or whatever name is given the Most High]? Why are people afraid of non-physical spirit beings? Why is it so hard to find spiritual peace, or joy, or harmony? The list can go on. Put in other sections which you know are important.

We suggest that you not do this exercise with all of these questions at once. Let Spirit lead you to several that are particularly interesting to you. Come back to the others at a later date.

141

The next statement is very important. If you want to participate in this process, stop reading now and do the exercise above. If you want to participate, but not now, skip the remainder of this section. Come back to it later, when you can write.

When you have given these questions some consideration, and have a full list, go back to the list and summarize each answer with a short phrase. For example. If you said people do not meditate because they do not have time, then summarize it by writing "Lack of time prevents meditation." Put these statements on the left side of a new piece of paper before reading further.

Now, let's reveal the nature of this exercise. The things you put down about what prevents others from succeeding in creating joy, peace, love, abundance and harmony, are the things that prevent *you*. These thoughts were in your mind, not others'. If others fill out the list, it may be different, but others did not, you did. You chose which sections you wanted to deal with. These choices came because Spirit in you wanted to address these issues. There are no accidents in life. All is in divine order.

Understand that your brain-mind works like a computer, garbage in, and garbage out. What you put out, is what has been put in; regardless of whether or not you agree this information fits the surface beliefs you have about yourself. Again, return to the story of the father and son in a car accident. You may not think of yourself as one who discriminates against women, but if you could not answer the question, you do.

So accept responsibility that these summarized statements you wrote down are imbedded in your subconscious mind. They are the hidden saboteurs that are robbing you of the full expression of your spiritual being.

So what do you do? First, decide if you want to do anything at all. You may not. If you do wish to address any of these items, then choose the section you wish to address. Take out the paper with the phrases written on it. Write affirmations on the right side that directly address each phrase.

The rules for writing effective affirmations are: First: The affirmation must be simple, exact and focused. Make it a phrase, or a very short sentence. Second: It must be a positive statement. Do not use negative words like 'not', 'try' or 'should'. Third: The affirmation is to be in the present tense. Fourth: Use actions statements when possible. 'I find I enjoy visualizations', is an example. Fifth: Use the word 'I' when you are going to say the affirmation. Use 'you' when you will listen to it. To listen to an affirmation, tape them on cassette tapes. You may wish to play meditation music with white noise in the background while you record. Sixth: Set attainable realistic affirmations. To do this, you sometimes have to use the back door approach. For example, if you do not feel you can accomplish something in your heart, even with the affirmation, then your heart will rule. Find a compromise that is less demanding, that you can believe. After this affirmation works, change the affirmation, make it reflect the desired outcome more. This may be a several-step process.

After you have made the affirmations, deal with only one issue at a time. Say the affirmation with passion as often as you can throughout the day. At least once a day say them with outrageous passion. Jump up and down, scream, declare to the universe that it is so. Passion is a driving force, an energy in motion, that makes it so.

If you make tapes, then listen to the affirmations (which are now called suggestions) while you meditate. Ear phones are especially useful. Some hints on making tapes are: record background meditation music on your suggestion tape about five to ten minutes before you begin; repeat your suggestions. Write as many versions of the same suggestion as you can, and record these versions.

While you are listening to the suggestions, visualize yourself surrounded by Light. Then see yourself engaging in the positive activity desired. This will greatly enhance the effect of the process. Even if you do not make tapes, you can still do the visualizations.

Another helpful hint is to engage in all affirmations with a prayerful mind. As you do this, you invite assistance from the many aspects of Spirit within and without. Without prayer, this technique has limitations. The suggestions, if not embedded deep enough into your subconscious mind, may wear off. However, with assistance from Spirit, it can be permanent.

Here is where the delicate balance must come in. It has been discussed earlier in the book about praying for issues. Many of the affirmations and suggestions you wrote will deal with clear cut issues. Reread the section on prayer in chapter two. Then decide how you want to use affirmations relative to where you are on your spiritual journey. Seek guidance from Spirit.

If you choose not to deal with certain revealed issues, this self sabotage experiment was still successful. You have revealed saboteurs in your life. By simply doing so you have placed them in the Light, and they can no longer hide. So now if these saboteurs show up to kill, steal and destroy, you know what to do. Remember the African ritual of speaking a positive thing into existence, and tell those saboteurs a thing or two.

Fear is one of the greatest saboteurs of all time. Fear is not always hidden. Fear is in your face. It stops supernatural events from happening, and can shut you down for years to come.

To understand how fear can creep into your life, and tear holes in our supernatural walk in Spirit, I will share a series of events that happened to me.

When I began my spiritual journey in my early adult years, I was so excited that even my sleep seemed electrified with energy. I would often wake up in the mornings strangely detached from my body. I was fully aware, thinking clearly, and in my body, but I could not move. It was awesome. I was like a child with a new toy.

Freedom of being, without the cumbersome body. Out of curiosity, I would often struggle to move, but I could not even budge a finger. Each time it happened, I would just lay on the bed enjoying it, and eventually I would somehow attach to my body, with the ability to move.

After this happened numerous times, someone told me if I said a prayer of protection, I would come out of it immediately. So the next several times it happened, I said a prayer, and I immediately gained control of my body.

Being armed with prayer, the idea of this total separation from mind and body became even more fascinating to me. I was now ready to boldly explore this strange new reality. At this time, I did not realize Spirit was re-introducing me to the out-of-body experiences I routinely enjoyed as a child. I stopped leaving my body as a child, because I was told I was crazy. I feared being crazy, so I stopped.

Now, back to the story. The next time I woke up and found myself detached, a bizarre journey unfolded. At first, I waited and waited anxiously for something to happen. Then suddenly in a flash, I found myself in a small rustic room, laying on a bed by an open window. The surroundings felt familiar, like it was my room, but I knew I had not been here in this life. Gale force winds were blowing outside, just inches away from where I lay. A piece of transparent plastic, nailed over the window, flapped in the wind so loudly it was almost deafening. As I gazed out the window, I had an eerie feeling that someone was outside the window, and they knew I was in the room. I beckoned them to reveal themselves, but they would not. So I continued to lay there in peace and serenity. But eventually the noise got so loud it became distracting. I said a prayer, and was instantly swept away from this curious place.

Thrilled by this weird experience, I longed to understand it. I openly told anyone who would listen. Then one day, as I told one lady, she looked at me with glazed eyes. I could tell the spirit of fear

145

had griped her very soul. In quivering voice she responded. "Don'
you know, the witches are riding your back." The energy of her fea
was contagious. Fear gripped me when she stated this old wives' tale
I opened myself to her suggestion, and doubt and apprehensio
penetrated to my very bones.

Later, I rationalized there was no reason to fear thes
experiences. So in time, I thought I had talked myself out of thi
foreboding feeling.

Then one morning, I woke up and tried to get out of bed,
could not move my legs. The experience was upon me. Immediately
I recalled the glazed over bulging eyes of the lady while she sai
"witches are riding your back." Thoughts raced through my head o
wicked, dark spirits, lurking over my body trying to suck the life ou
of me. Terror ripped through every part of my being. I franticall
tried to move. The harder I tried, the more frightened I became. I
felt like the angel of death was knocking at my door. Then it came t
me, just say a prayer. I prayed, and immediately, I jumped out of bec
in a cold sweat.

Since that day seventeen years ago, I have not had thi
experience again. I let fear rob me of this wondrous feeling o
freedom twice. Once as a child, and once as an adult.

I now know witches were not riding my back. I know thes
experiences were just another form of out-of-body training I wa
going through.

Fear is one of the most devastating deterrents to experiencin
supernatural events. Fear is a thief that robs you of your spiritua
power, wisdom and heritage. Fear prevents you from becoming wh
you truly are.

Many people cringe at the thought of a spirit being appearin
in their bedroom at night. Unfortunately, most people have beer
programmed by society and television to fear any living being tha
does not have a physical body. We all were told spooky bed-tim

146

ghost stories when we were children. We were indoctrinated to blindly fear ghosts, goblins and witches, which translates in a child's mind as any being without physical form.

As you evolve in Spirit, you will open up to other worlds, dimensions and realities. You will discover that you do reside in dimensions other than the physical. You will eventually encounter beings of light, angels and spirit guides. However, if you carry the childhood fear of creepy, crawly things in the night, you may just shut yourself down to these beings. To grow spiritually, one must be rid of all fears.

To overcome fear of the supernatural world, engage in fervent prayer and meditation without an agenda of receiving anything, but divine love. Perfect love will cast out all fear. Surround yourself with light as often as you can. Seek out friends and mentors who experience and discuss supernatural events as part of their normal conversation. This will help you become comfortable with the paranormal.

We strongly suggest you stop watching horror movies, or any program, or book that deals with the dark side. There is no need to continue to fill your consciousness with this negativity.

I have talked to many people who had a visitation while in meditation, and the visitation scared them right out of the meditation, and the experience. Always remember, if you have a visitation, and you feel reluctant, just ask the being, "are you of the Most High Spirit?" If the being is not, then be assured, it cannot stay, and it will flee. It can be as simple as that. (Read the section 'Emotions and feeling that cause stress' in the Stress chapter.)

One must realize the Most High Spirit does not dwell in the separating energy of fear. Part of growing into divinity with the All In All is to practice the presence of the beings of light. These beings are essential. They teach us, impart gifts into us, and guide us back home. As you seek Spirit first and foremost, your spiritual vibration is increased. This increased energy allows your conscious to expand and enables it to perceive beings in other realms. If fear is in your heart, these divine visitors know this, and may refrain from scaring you by not showing themselves to you. You would clearly be the loser in this situation.

Remember Spirit, which is in you, is omnipotent. The truth of being one with this omnipotent Spirit sets up a protection that nothing can penetrate. So have faith. Besides, it is all in divine order.

If you fear, doubt or worry, you alienate yourself from the divine source you are trying to return to. You may end up feeling lonely, like a man living on a deserted island. The very act of fear, may even bring to you that which you fear most.

As you are willing to face your fear, you will discover the common saying about fear is true. FEAR is 'False Evidence Appearing Real'. Cast fear to the side, and open up. You will then be uninhibited to experience supernatural events that are so magnificent that words cannot adequately explain them.

Understanding supernatural events that words cannot explain is a real dilemma in spiritual education. The unexplainable events are numerous. They may include out-of-body experiences, becoming one with a tree or bird, rolling over into another person's body, closing your eyes and seeing far-off, distant lands, tasting the food another is eating, receiving physical nourishment from energy, or even making love to a star. If you have had one of these experiences with full awareness, you do not have to wonder about it. It was so real, and so different, and so undeniable that you know it happened. However, if you tried to explain one of these experiences to a person unfamiliar with spirituality, they might look at you like you are crazy.

Herein lies a dilemma. A spiritual master cannot share her spiritual reality with individuals less spiritually developed. This is because her reality is incomprehensible. It defies human logic, reason, and beliefs.

The best way to understand the awesome task that lies before a spiritual master trying to explain the spiritual life is to imagine yourself in a similar situation. Here is good example. Imagine you have discovered a small tribe of indigenous people who have never been exposed to modern man. They live a simple life off the land, hunting and gathering. They have no written language or mentionable technology. The only tools are beautifully designed hunting spears.

Now imagine trying in one afternoon, or even one week, explaining the basics of modern culture, and its technologies to them. This includes automobiles, airplanes, television, radio, electricity and common household appliances. You must explain that people do not hunt and gather. They have the 40 hour work week in which they make money. Money buys their food from a grocery store. Also you must explain the system of educating children that takes 12 to 20 years [if one gets a doctorate]. This discussion includes not only writing, but the many courses and majors one can specialize in, such as electrical engineering or sociology. Now imagine doing this and you don't even speak the same language. The task is impossible.

Even if you learned their language, and spent a year living with them, the task would still be impossible. The reality in your world has so many variables and complexities it would be incomprehensible to them. For them to truly comprehend your world, they must leave the [false] security of their forest home, and journey with you to the city.

A spiritual master has the same problem. The spirit world has so many variables and complexities that even if you sat at the feet of a master for years and heard her explain it, it would still be incomprehensible. For you to truly comprehend this spirit world, you must leave the false security of your physical world, and journey into Spirit.

The sad report is that most people on the spiritual path are just sitting at the feet of a master (the Higher Nature within) trying to glean what Spirit is. They are afraid to leave the security of the world between their ears. They are afraid to do what it takes to become serious about spirit. So what are these things that one must do?

To start the real spiritual journey, it is best for to get it right, right where their consciousness is. This includes living in the present, divorcing yourself from outcomes, reducing expectations, increasing acceptance, stop judging; forgiving, and releasing needs. This means you put Spirit first. Not your pain. Not your current crisis. Not your self-pity. Not your past suffering as a child. Not your desires to find a group or church that fits with your philosophical belief. Not your insatiable appetite to read spiritual books, or go to seminars and workshops.

These are the beginning rules for moving out of physical reality into Spiritual reality. Many desire the great spiritual experiences, but do not want to do the foundation work.

Of course, you can learn to develop specific spiritual abilities and have selected experiences. You can take all kinds of workshops and classes that teach everything under the sun. Many experience these supernatural events naturally. They have done nothing, and they just have all kinds of experiences. However, these spiritual abilities without love, peace and wisdom, are shallow technologies and will never deliver you into wholeness.

Spiritual ability to some is like a radio to forest people. It is a beautiful gift, but is will not shelter them in a storm; feed them when they are hungry; or comfort them in times of pain. You can spend your energy acquiring spiritual abilities, and running after spiritual experiences; or you can spend your energy moving into the oneness of Spirit. If you choose the latter, all of the spiritual abilities will eventually be yours. Then you might discover that the need for spiritual abilities, or anything, vanishes.

Needing spiritual abilities is one of the traps on the spiritual path. Many individuals believe if they do not have, or acquire spiritual abilities, they are not growing spiritually. So they need spiritual abilities and supernatural events.

Need opens the door to fear; fear that you will not have the supernatural things or events needed. Fear is doubt, and doubt is the opposite of faith. Without faith drawing the supernatural things to you, your supernatural experiences will decrease.

The basic message is not to have supernatural needs. You may exercise certain abilities, or even nurture their onset, but do not feel you need them to be whole. When spiritual events or abilities do occur, sincerely give thanks to Spirit within and without with all your heart.

Thanks giving makes supernatural events happen. Giving thanks is an act of faith. If you need $100, you may choose to tell a friend. If the friend responded, "I will give you the money," you would immediately thank the friend, even though the friend does not have the money at that moment. You have faith that the friend is good for his word. You expressed that faith by a statement of gratitude.

A statement of gratitude before a thing manifests is a statement of faith. Faith attracts to you that which is desired. So sincerely give thanks for all things. For ultimately you desire to have all things in oneness.

Upon giving thanks, do not forget to give thanks to yourself. Not in an ego pleasing way, but in a way to identify yourself with the Spirit that lies within.

There is an exquisite balance that must be found in thanks giving. Spirit, the Most High, is your Creator, your ultimate mentor, your mother and father, your All In All. However, this Spirit is in you, what you are, and who you are. If you view Spirit as being separate from you, with all accolades and thanks giving to Spirit without, you have trapped yourself into a thought process in the world of duality. God above, man below. However, if your thought process is that the Most High Spirit dwells within, and you focus all of your attention on your God nature, you have again trapped yourself in the world of duality. God within, and not without.

The ultimate way to avoid this trap, which seems to sometimes be our only frame of reference, is to remember oneness. To remember oneness, we must believe in our hearts this is possible. As you believe this, you begin to know it. If you know this, then give thanks. Thank kind Spirit within and without for allowing your consciousness to be increased to recall all things.

Other principles on opening to supernatural events are important. These concepts have been discussed in detail in other parts of the book. Nonetheless, some of these concepts in review are: Be open for spiritual guidance in everything. Be obedient to Spirit's guidance. Be quick to listen, to feel, to sense, to know; but slow to speak. Hold little stock in your old thoughts of reason, and question work. Trust the thoughts of Spirit within. Give others advice as Spirit directs. Know you are one with Spirit. Stop lusting, and eliminate worry. Stop struggling, flow naturally with the unctions of Spirit. When you do these things, and the things within this chapter, you will begin to awaken to universal consciousness - the source of all supernatural events.

For in universal consciousness, miracles occur, healing takes place, and supernatural events are daily experiences. When you are one in the present moment with Spirit, there is a clear knowing that there is no division between Spirit, your desires, and the supernatural. As you open yourself without limitation, all things you require are yours. Things and events are attracted to you by absolute faith.

The need to ask vanishes completely, because you know you are the center of Divine law in action, a law of absolute abundance on all levels of existence. Your unlimited consciousness has expanded and knows your every desire. Your wishes and dreams are supplied simply because you are. Perfect fulfillment in heavenly places is your

152

birthright; instant creation on all levels of existence your way of life, even creation of physical material, right out of thin air.

The truly evolved masters know they are the focal point for whatever needs to manifest, and things natural and supernatural automatically come. Thus, a need is not a lack, but an opportunity to grow within by receiving all that is good. The master no longer struggles. Everything is a natural flow of grace. She is one with the One. A part of the Source, omnipotent, omniscient, and omnipresent.

Thank you kind Spirit.

Common Sense Exercise: Feeling Energy.

If you have not experienced feeling the human energy field, this is a supernatural - really natural - thing you can do right now. Call several people together. Some male and some female. Then take turns feeling each others energy field or aura. Stand arm's-length away from your partner. Extend your arm straight out to your side, shoulder height. Then slowly move your hands toward your partner's head. You will feel your partner's energy field before your hands touch her\his head. Next, try to explain what it feels like.

After you do this, get another partner of the opposite sex. Feel their energy field in the same manner. Note how the energy field of a male feels different from that of a female. Try to explain this difference.

Finally, place your hands within someone's energy field. Feel the entire energy field that surrounds their whole body, and look for any difference. This can be done by slowly running your hands over their entire body, without touching them. If you feel a difference in the energy emission, it is often associated with an energy blockage, illness or problem. Ask the person if there are any problems in this area.

By practicing this simple technique, you will improve your ability to feel energy. In time you will be able to easily pick up a stressed or blocked area in a person's body.

Thank you kind Spirit.

Chapter 6

Spiritual Concepts Made Clear

Love: the way to spiritual success.

Your birthright is unconditional, intimate love. What would you do if you could absolutely trust your life would be filled with love and prosperity? What if you could believe you are always safe and protected? Imagine how you could move in life. Your fears would disappear. You would always know you are successful. Unconditional acceptance of yourself and others would be easy. You would be free to experience the fullness of life.

In the physical world, this magnitude of success is not possible. You reap what you sow. But as you leave the physical in conscious awareness, and walk in Spirit, you can reap where you have not sown. You can experience the fullness of infinite love.

Love is the most important virtue that humans have. It molds us, binds us together, nurtures our wounds, and caresses our spirits. It is the glue that holds the fabric of the universe together. As we find true unconditional love, we find the hidden treasure of the universe. We find the very essence of the Most High Spirit.

Love in Spirit is indescribable; its expressions and characteristics are clear. Love is kind, gentle and patient. Love endures all things, believes all things, and aspires to all things. Love does not envy, is not vain or dangerous to others. Love does not rejoice in iniquity, but rejoices in truth. Where there is love, there is increase. Where there is love, there is unity. Where there is love, there is oneness.

True success is the discovery that unconditional love of Spirit is in us. We don't know this in the natural world because we lack the consciousness to experience it. However, there is an inner voice that keeps calling us to connect with our true and Higher Nature.

As you form a habit of being obedient to your inner voice, a wonderful, upward spiral of success will appear in your life. As success comes, your confidence in Spirit will begin to soar. Confidence will expand your vision of what can be accomplished on the spiritual path. This ever increasing vision will gradually bring you to a place of realizing how intimate your daily walk with Spirit can be, and your desire to know Spirit will increase. As you open yourself to know Spirit, love will come into your heart, because the Most High Spirit is love. As love saturates your being, your love for Spirit will increase your desire to please Spirit and be obedient. Then, the cycle of obedience, confidence, vision and love repeats itself, and your consciousness expands more.

As your consciousness expands by Spirit, you begin to walk in the divine love that is Spirit. Divine love uplifts you, and all that it contacts. This is the nature of this hidden treasure. Its very essence attracts prosperity, peace, harmony and joy. As you become a magnet for all things, success comes to you without effort. You reap where you have not sown.

There are no short cuts on this path of love and success. This cycle of love does not work for many because they never get past the first step of obedience. Man has a will, and as long as man's will is alive and undisciplined, it will be followed, instead of the gentle instructions of the feminine still, small voice.

The will of man is strange but interesting. It is self destructive; its nature is not love. It simply desires to consume and accumulate all it can, including your sanity; it has a ravenous appetite, always wanting more, never willing to stop; it always drives you to follow its mandates, which are programmed by an unforgiving culture which has taught us to look outside of ourselves for validation and happiness.

Do you care for yourself? Do you take time for yourself? Do you honor your needs? Or, do you always live outside of yourself, trying to be a good parent, a good spouse, a good employee, a good friend? Is your daily life so full of working and doing things for others, that you never do for yourself?

Your acts send messages to your spirit. Your body is a holy temple that you have been entrusted with. Do you care for it? Honor it? Sanctify it? Do you treat it as the precious gift that it is? Or, do you deny it rest and sleep, to get a little more accomplished? Do you habitually overeat?

If you do not take time to fulfill the needs of body, mind and spirit, then disharmony and disease overtakes you. Feelings of emptiness, dissatisfaction, depression or loneliness creep in.

To have a successful life, you must care for yourself; pamper yourself; take time to be with yourself. You must love yourself.

Love of self is the starting point for love of others. If your cup is half empty, you cannot fill another's cup. If you are constantly stressed, depressed and angry with life, you cannot be a blessing to others. So, in order to think clearly, act wisely, pray sincerely, you must defuse the stresses of the day. You must take time for self.

Taking time for self could mean relaxing in an herbal bath, walking in the park or just going into a room and closing the door. We all intuitively know the importance of caring for self. However, doing it is another thing. We have been conditioned to think this is selfish or vain. Self-love is not vain. Self-love starts by being kind to yourself; not beating up on yourself for every situation and dilemma, respecting your thoughts; enjoying being with yourself; knowing that you are beautiful; taking time to listen to yourself and heal yourself.

Self love is ultimately being willing to devote your entire being to spiritual evolution.

A good way to know if you are caring for yourself properly, is to ask yourself these questions. Are you as loving to yourself and your needs as you would be to your child? How many times have you denied yourself something that you would give a loved one? Is getting the job done more important than staying healthy? How often are you depressed? Are you over - or under - eating? Are you eating correctly? Do you have time, or take time, to meditate and exercise? Does your self-esteem ever suffer? Are you over stressed? Are you ill? Do you become ill?

Nurturing and caring for yourself will give you the ability to eat properly. It will provide the energy to exercise, and the time to meditate. It will ease self-doubt, and promote self-acceptance. Develop personal rituals to honor the divine being that you are. Congratulate yourself throughout the day for each accomplishment you make. Recall each time you chose to be calm and at peace, instead of rushed and stressed, and then compliment yourself on a job well done. Always remember to thank Spirit for allowing the expression of self-love.

If you are willing to live in the present, celebrate life, work on yourself, submit to Spirit, and try love, you will discover something along your success journey. You will discover love is a magnet that draws abundance from all levels of existence. You will discover an unimaginable sense of joy as you awaken to the pure and perfect love of Spirit within. Through experience, you will learn that the ultimate success in life is unconditional love of self, others, and Spirit. You will discover love is truly who and what you are.

Thank you kind Spirit.

Spiritual Seasons: How to discern and awaken in them.

Different energies rain into Mother Earth at different times, creating shifts in the spiritual air, and cycles of seasons. These shifts and spiritual seasons range from split moments in time, to billions of years.

An essential key to spiritual evolution and manifestation is the ability to discern spiritual seasons. It would be foolish to plant seeds in early winter. It is also foolish to undertake certain spiritual growth processes in the incorrect spiritual season. Specific spiritual growth initiations must be conducted in appropriate spiritual seasons to reap maximum success.

There are two basic types of spiritual seasons. Those affecting Mother Earth, and all her inhabitants, and the unique spiritual timing and internal seasons within each person. It is equally important to be able to discern internal seasons as well as the universal seasons.

The study of Astrology is one quick way to understand spiritual seasons. The alignment of stars and planets is a physical indicator of spiritual seasons. Additionally, the pure spiritual science of Astrology can provide information as to what to do in a particular season to maximize spiritual growth.

However, a major problem with modern Astrology is that much of it has been commercialized and distorted, as many major religions have been.

Most modern Astrology has been written, learned and handed down in the context of what has popular appeal. What can sell is best. It has also been handed down in the context of the mind of man and manipulated. This masculine-dominated mind functions out of lust, lack and fear; a mind that sees the cup half empty instead of half full; a mind that focuses on the natural world, and not the supernatural; a mind that has made Astrology a god. The daily newspaper horoscope -rooted in physical world events - is an obvious indication. A less obvious example of this is an Astrologer telling you that Mercury is in retrograde, then warns you not to sign contracts. This kind of fear based information provides limited guidance for the serious student of spirituality.

I have met only a few spiritual Astrologers who have discarded this form of prediction, and truly place this sacred tool in the spiritual context of consistently assisting others in an optimistic approach to spiritual evolution. Fortunately, discerning the spiritual seasons can involve more than just Astrology. Some spiritually advanced people regularly receive knowledge of the spiritual seasons, and how to maximize their work during this particular season.

When I first discovered that some people had the gift of discerning seasons and simultaneously knowing what to do, I found myself validating their teachings. I would listen to them; then listen to several others. Without fail, their reports were the same, but with the following exception. Many modern Astrologers reported from a limited, physical world, and often fear based perspective. The spiritually receptive individuals, seeking love, almost always gave the report from an optimistic point of view.

Love is an important side point. Many spiritually open but fear based individuals always predicted physical world doom and gloom. If you are not a true seeker of love, your vision will be clouded.

Now back to Astrology. This is not an attempt to bash Astrology. Astrology is an intricately beautiful spiritual system which, used correctly, can be a helpful tool on our path to ascension. However, I hope this report will challenge Astrologers to re-evaluate their books, tools and teachings, and bring the tool of Astrology back into alignment with the greater purpose of life. To evolve into the creator beings of love and light that we are is the life purpose of each and every human.

After years of validating, comparing and following the spiritual seasons, I discovered something else that was equally interesting. Discerning the spiritual seasons is a natural and normal process that any student of spirituality can perform. It is not as hard as one would suspect. In fact, you and just about everyone else is doing it right now. It is a documented fact that during a full moon more crimes are committed, and there are more visits to the hospital emergency room. Just as more people commit crimes and get sick, you too, are feeling these shifts. You just may not have realized it.

The first step in discerning the seasons is to pay attention to what is happening inside you. An energy shift may be the cause of a shift in the nature of your daily meditations. If you feel unusually sensitive, happy, confident, or sad, for no apparent reason, you are probably feeling an energy shift. Next, immediately call several of your spiritual friends and ask them how they are feeling. If they are feeling the same types of things, you can be sure it is an energy shift.

Also, watch for changes in your environment. If suddenly everything seems to be going smoothly and working out, or if struggles abruptly appear from nowhere, then pool several of your spiritual colleagues and see if the same thing is happening to them.

Pooling with your colleagues has benefits other than the obvious. It validates in your consciousness that you are sensing various types of energy changes and increases your trust and faith that you can do this. Pooling also increases your awareness of energy changes, or internal shifts in your spirit or physiology. If your colleagues do not sense a change, do not discount what you are feeling. The shift may be an internal one.

In time, you will become very clear on the daily and weekly energy shifts that are coming into Mother Earth. As you become better at discerning these shifts, you will begin to discern longer spiritual seasons. Look for these longer seasons to last for months, years and decades.

As you get an inkling of a longer spiritual season, continue the validation process. Ask Astrologers what season you are in. Also ask or observe other spiritual groups to see if they are aware of the current spiritual season. When you ask these questions, you must understand that other groups probably speak a different language than you. Obviously, an Astrologer might tell you of the planetary alignments, then explain and define how it is affecting your relationships. You may have to read between the lines if Spirit gave you information in a different way.

When you are talking to other spiritual groups, be very open. Most people have problems hearing the truth in another person's reality because of philosophical differences. For example, there are a few Christian ministries that know exactly what season we are in, and exactly what to do in the season. Some New Age believers feel the Christian doctrine is inferior.

First of all, doctrine is not spirituality. Even if you disagree with a person's doctrine, that person can bring forth wisdom shaded by the color of their doctrine. If you can read between the lines, and remain open and confident enough to let Spirit within you discern the truth from another's shaded reality, you are much better off. Be careful not to get involved in trying to correct others' views unless they ask for help. This only creates confusion and tension.

Learning to discern seasons is the first part. Next you must be open to receive from Spirit how to maximize your growth in the present season. Interesting events occur as you start discerning the seasons, and as you desire to grow, Spirit will direct you. Even if you feel you have not yet established a direct line, that is, you do not hear a voice, or receive detailed knowings, Spirit will tell you indirectly. Your revelations may come in dreams, coincidences, or synchronistic actions of others. Trust that this information will come, and be open to receive it from any source.

You may find it helpful to ask other spiritual groups what they are doing in a given season. Again, be open to read between the lines. To make it clear how one must read between the lines, let us look at a real example. This example also shows how an optimistic approach can be found in even the most outwardly depressing seasons.

Several years ago there was a season in which every foul characteristic was seemingly rising to the surface. Tempers were flaring, anger was present in the workplace, and at home. A general sense of insanity was in the air. So one's first question was, what could one possibly do in a season like this, except try to stay calm? There is plenty one could do. Some Christian communities considered this a time of deliverance and many engaged in deliverance services.

Deliverance is a process of casting demonic spirits out of people. During this season, many seemingly dark spirits were clearly surfacing in people, and these people were delivered. There is another way to look at this doctrine-laden practice. This was a season in which the suffering of your ancestors and past incarnations could easily express itself on the surface. This surfacing energy brought pain, misery and insanity into your present incarnation. These past souls were in desperate need of a healing. So this was a time to intentionally let this energy come full circle to the surface. For when it was on the surface, intense Light could be directly administered to it for the purpose of healing and renewing.

In this spiritual season, I found more Christian ministries that knew what to do than other spiritual groups. Astrological readings simply indicated it was a difficult period. Consequently, many spiritually tuned people chose to just ride this season out, and wait until it ended. However, they missed an opportunity to become captain of their ships, and heal the lost souls within. If these groups would have observed the Christians without judgment, they may have been led by Spirit to appropriate actions for their ancestors in this season.

163

Regardless to how you approached this season, casting out demons or healing past wounded and suffering incarnations, the results were the same. You were freed to evolve to another level of spirituality. One doctrine and approach may feel more accurate than another, but if you were not open to the truth from another spiritual system, you could have missed it all together.

Now this brings us to one of the most profound and wonderful things about spiritual seasons. If you can ride the spiritual waves of energy that flow into Mother Earth, you can effortlessly sail from glory to glory. Every spiritual season offers a glory or victory to be achieved. This glory can be an increase in a wavelength in your spiritual vibration. Each season has a glory or vibration associated with it. As you receive the glory of that season, and ride to the next one in grace, your return to your divine creative self will be easier.

The key is to know when to move from one glory to the next. When a season changes, you may no longer need the past glory. Holding on to the old glory may prevent you from focusing on and receiving a new one.

During the so-called deliverance season, I encountered individuals that rose to a new level of energy. They were efficient channels who could deliberately pull the dark forces to the surface in other people, and then send Light to free them. As this season passed, if these individuals held on to this glorious gift, and tried to deliver everyone they came in contact with, they would have been carrying excess baggage. This gift works best in a given season, and outside of this season its use may move against the current of new energy. One must be as freely willing to drop a glory, as they are to pick it up. Spirit will lead you how and when to do this.

Unfortunately, many people are afraid to release an ability once they receive it. This is because they fear losing it forever. Fear is not of the Most High Spirit. This energy ultimately damages

164

growth. Besides, a fascinating thing happens when one relinquishes a glory in due season: it can be picked up again if truly needed.

One final note about spiritual seasons. Some spiritual seasons seem to be great times of increase. Everything is happening that causes balance, peace, harmony and prosperity. During these seasons one can increase their spiritual vibration to help carry them through dry seasons, where finding balance is harder, manifesting is a struggle, and peace seems elusive. Even though all seasons have a purpose and an associated blessing, storing up energy during the increasing times will help one through the droughts.

This leads us to one of the most mysteriously magnificent truths within Spirit. To convey this point, I will transcribe a direct message that was channeled through me, for me.

> *"You see my child, there will be times in which you will be required to go into the desert. In these dry places you will come into the fullness that your are. You will develop into who I am. One with me. One with the Christ. Your full glory as a Star Light. In these times you will not be setting in heavenly places. Grace will not abound. In these times you must make the matrix. Find your way home, and bless the areas you are in with great Light. These are the times of creation. For in the void of nothingness I created all heaven and earth. This void was the desert without grace. Without the matrix of synchronicity. You my child must do the same. As you go into hell and redeem the souls that are there, you gain the experience of the creator being that you are."*

Know this: all things are in divine order. For even in the darkest season there is Light. The ultimate is to have your energy so high, that you bring this Light to any season under the sun.

Thank you kind Spirit.

Spiritual Initiations: What to Expect?

Did you know that your entire journey back to oneness is one long spiritual initiation? However, for the purpose of this book, we will reduce it to smaller ones.

A spiritual initiation is any series of events that result from your desire to move into Spirit. Spiritual initiations are as much a part of spiritual growth, as air is a part of breathing. These initiations bring you closer to your Higher Nature. One must go through spiritual initiations to awaken and evolve in Spirit. True initiations are one of the most underrated events in the spiritual community. People do not teach or deal with them, because they are not always easy.

An initiation occurs for a combination of reasons. We consciously or subconsciously seek initiation: to receive a victory, glory or spiritual ability; to flow with the energy of a season; to spark your forgetfulness into remembrance; to end the feelings of separation and return to oneness; to discipline, die to, or awaken from, the ego driven masculine will of man. These are just a few reasons for spiritual initiations.

In spiritual initiations, expect the unexpected. If you know everything that is going to happen, when it's going to happen, and how it's going to happen, it's not an initiation. It's an act of discipline.

In spiritual initiations, you sometimes have help or facilitators. The assistance can be directly from Spirit guiding you through the initiation. The initiations can be facilitated by a manifestation of Spirit in the form of a spirit guide, ancestor or angel. You can be initiated by an individual or an organization.

Many organizational initiations originated from Spirit, and were handed down through the generations as rituals. Some of the rituals today are only types and shadows of the original initiations. In addition, many of these rituals have become part of man's institutions to confer degrees, certificates or honors. This is designed to boost one's ego, status or self esteem. It may also allow one to make money under the auspices of the certification. These types of initiations have little merit with Spirit. If you are initiated by a person that has come up with the initiation independent of the inspiration of Spirit, then you are being initiated by man, and not by Spirit. The initiations of man may not have spiritual significance. But they will almost always have a certificate, degree or honor.

Do not get caught in the trap of certificates and honors. These may be nice to have, but the time you waste getting man's approval may not be worth it. Spend your time wisely. Seek after the initiations of Spirit. These are the ones that will transform you. The ones that eliminate worry, pain and distress. These are the ones that will increase your consciousness, and make a difference in your spiritual evolution.

Spiritual initiations take many forms. They may be a simple act of losing a precious item, releasing it, and then finding it with the help of Spirit. In the Bible, Job lost everything he had, including his health. When he refused to curse God, he regained it all in twice the measure.

Spiritual initiations can happen with or without your knowledge. As one becomes more advanced in sensing the shift of energy, one knows when an initiation is upon them. This, however, does not make the initiation any easier. An undisciplined mind unknowingly creates stressful circumstances that will eventually initiate you from its clutches. What a marvelous concept Spirit has devised! This concept is dealt with in great detail in the chapter on how stress saves our souls.

Initiations are often dramatic. For instance, Spirit may catch you off-guard, and with a loud voice echoing in your mind ask: "What do you want; anything you ask for is yours." Any answer you give

The Common Sense Guide for Spirituality

ill have a heart-rending effect on you. For example, if in your heart ou may immediately answer something like: "To know you." Then ou may get an answer from Spirit like: "Well done my child, I pprove." But if you hesitate, and engage your rational mind before nswering, you may not get a response at all. Spirit is after your eart, not your mind. But suppose you gave a heart-felt instant nswer and said: "I want a new car." You may get a new car, but iiss an opportunity of a lifetime - an opportunity to come closer to ie Source where all abundance resides. Incidentally, I have talked to everal people who had this initiatory question asked of them.

During spiritual initiations, always seek a lesson. As in the bove example, you can learn a lesson regardless to how you answer he question. If you hesitated to answer, you should realize you still ely on your rational mind to move. The rational mind of man will get ou nowhere fast on your spiritual journey. You need to pray, isualize and meditate to release this mind, and open your heart. If ou asked for material goods, then Spirit is not foremost in your heart. o grow to all that you can be, Spirit must be first and foremost. A rayer for sincerity would be in order.

Initiations can be cyclic, like being brainwashed for a period of ime to shift your thinking process, then being guided to another way f thinking, only to eventually return to your former beliefs. This is lone to shift or change a faulty foundation. The layers on the oundation had to be removed before the building could be replaced. An example of a cyclic initiation is given below in the discussion of group initiations.

Group initiations are often one of the most profound forms of nitiation. I was part of a cyclic group initiation which lasted over two years. The initiator was Spirit speaking through one person. She lirectly initiated one individual and finally initiated the group. During hose two years we were asked to believe in our heart concepts that eemed to go against all of our former thinking. We were actually told to dismiss all that we knew about masculine and feminine energy. We were given new information such as: there is nothing good about a man; every thought a man has is evil; a man - the masculine will - must die. These concepts were drilled into us weekly. They were to almost became our mantras. They were to be our every thought, and consume our lives. Then upon believing, we were required to act on this new information. Men were required to confess their transgressions publicly; be totally submissive and obedient to the feminine, usually a wife or girlfriend. Then and only then did the fruits of our labor become apparent. We discovered we were becoming balanced with the masculine and feminine energies. This was one of my most powerful initiations. It totally and completely changed my spiritual evolution, and launched me into another level of awakening. I am glad I had the courage to trust.

Going through this initiation required us to trust not only Spirit, but the channel for Spirit. Trust is an absolute necessity in initiations. You will never subject yourself to the fullness of the initiation if you do not have faith that all is working for the good of those that love Spirit.

Remember kind Spirit does not send you through hard times. If you are going through a situation that appears to be a crisis, it may be an initiation. Hard times, or the perception of hard times, come upon you because you created them knowingly, or unknowingly. Most often this is created because of your thought forms of unbalanced energy. Whatever the source of this energy, be it perceived as self, family, ancestors, or incarnations, take responsibility for it. Recognize everything is in divine order. Be patient. Be committed to evolve. Always have an attitude of gratitude.

You do not have to go out and look for a spiritual initiation. They are all around you. As you become committed to finding the true essence of Spirit within and without, you will go through growth enhancing initiations. A good place to start your commitment is fasting, sincere prayer, faithful meditation, and avidly seeking the highest good in all that you do. When seeking the highest good, in spiritual initiations, one thing is constant. As you make it through, your very spirit has changed and evolved. You may not be consciously aware of it, and it may take years for you to discern the change, but you have changed.

Knowing that you have been changed is reason to rejoice. So enjoy the journey of life and thank Spirit for it. Life is truly a miraculous blessing.

Thank you Kind Spirit.

Fasting for spiritual growth.

There are two categories of fasting. The first is denial, and second is moving faster toward Spirit. Denial fasting has limited spiritual rewards. This kind of fasting does have positive effects on the body-mind connection. It cleanses the physical body, and slows down and clears the mind.

Fasting for the purpose of moving faster toward Spirit has major results on spiritual growth. If this kind of fast is done correctly, it quickens the spirit, purges unbalanced energies within, and positively affects the physical, mental and emotional bodies. Increased visions, spiritual clarity, and enhanced dream recall are all benefits of repetitively fasting toward Spirit. This fast also ushers one into a closer personal relationship with Spirit, and assists in awakening one's Higher Nature; thereby, increasing discernment, wisdom, love, compassion, balance and power.

The way to fast toward Spirit is as follows: First broaden your concept of fasting. A fast can be anything from total abstinence of all ingested items, to skipping desert at one meal. To effectively fast toward Sprit, you must be unctioned (led) into a fast by Spirit. Let Spirit dictate the type of fast, and its duration. Then follow the instructions completely.

You may be unctioned into a fast in several different ways. You may be guided into the fast by a spiritual mentor or spiritually advanced trusted friend. Or you may get a clear cut message from Spirit as to when to start, stop, and what to consume, such as water or fresh juices. When this explicit type of instruction comes, follow it explicitly. However, being unctioned into a fast is often quite subtle. For example: one day "out of the blue" you may think about fasting, and in a casual conversation someone else might mention fasting. Then that afternoon, you find you are not hungry. Be quick to discern that you are [probably] being unctioned into a fast, so don't eat. A clear sign you have entered into the fast correctly is that when Spirit unctions you into a fast like this, the fast is as easy as riding a bike. You will not get excessively tired, and you just won't be hungry. You might desire to eat out of habit, but with a little discipline this is easily overcome.

Upon entering a fast like this, be open to receive when the fast should stop. The sign to stop may be as subtle as dreaming you are eating or hungry, to just simply having strong hunger pains or excessive fatigue. It is very important that you end a fast when unctioned. Extending the fast could be extremely damaging to the body. I have known of situations where individuals were unctioned into fasting, and out of ego they decided how many days they were going to fast. This is a mistake. If you were not given the number of hours or days, then be prepared to stop at any time. On the other hand, I have seen individuals unctioned into a fast, which lasted over two weeks, without any effort.

Many writings suggest fasts of many days with only water are best for spiritual enlightenment. This is true in many cases, but actually the best fast for spiritual enlightenment is the one Spirit unctions you into. When you are led into a fast by Spirit, benefits will be maximized. This is an indication that something inside is ready to move to the next level. The Spirit-lead fast will create the perfect environment to deliver you to the next level.

As fasting becomes an accepted and welcomed part of your life, be open to receive longer and more involved fasts. This will happen as your vessel becomes prepared to receive a greater influx of energy to maintain these prolonged fasts. When it comes to prolonged fasts like 21 days, or even short fasts like one day, most people have mental blocks. It is hard for one to conceive of not eating for prolonged periods of time. The question that often pops into one's consciousness is: Will I be riddled with hunger pains? Will I

173

get sick? Will I have enough energy to work? Or simply, it's just too hard!

It is important to get over this fear, because it will prevent you from receiving and following with the unction of Spirit. Like any fear, the way to work through it is to face it and embrace it. So, to get over this block, it is suggested that you enter into several fasts of your own volition. By doing several small fasts you will come to the realization that it is not as difficult as you imagined.

Start with doing a couple of one-day fasts, and then proceed to a three day fast. Separate these fasts by one week. The day preceding each fast, significantly reduce or delete meat consumption. During the fast it is recommended that you drink freshly juiced vegetable, and fruit juice, and plenty of water. The first day after the fast only eat small portions of soft vegetables and fruit. Do not eat dairy products or meats. It should take as many days to come of the fast as you spent on the fast. For example on the three-day fast, take three days to gradually return to your normal diet. This is extremely important. I have met many, myself included, who did not come off a fast gradually. After my first three-day fast, I went to an Italian restaurant and ate a big plate of linguine. I suffered with severe stomach cramps and pain for hours.

After fasting for three days, your digestive system shuts down. Therefore you must gradually introduce food back to it.

You will be interested to know that it is universally reported that after the first three days, the fasting becomes progressively easier.

During the fast, it is important to be positive and self-assured. Do not engage in complaining or self-pity. This will make the journey agonizingly painful. Remember this is a wonderful journey toward Spirit. Do it with a sense of joy and expectation. Increase your daily prayer and meditation. Rest more. Sleep more. Take it easy. Do not engage in overly strenuous exercise or activity. In other words, create the time to enjoy the experience.

174

It is also recommended that you buy another reference book on fasting. Find a book which gives details such as what to do if you have side effects during the fast, like headaches or gas. These side effects can be eliminated by drinking specific kinds of vegetable or fruit juices.

A final warning, if you have a health problem, like diabetes, which requires eating on regular intervals, you should not engage in the above exercise without your physician's approval.

Regardless of one's health issues there are many fasts that one can engage in. Remember the first rule of being unctioned into a fast is to broaden one's concept of fasting. Abstaining from food is only one narrow form of fasting. Anything that Spirit unctions you to omit, in order to move faster toward Spirit, can be considered a fast. For the purpose of this discussion, three forms of fasting will be considered. They are a silence fast, positive talk fast, and television news fast.

A silence fast means you choose not to talk, sing or otherwise utter any sounds for a given period of time. In a silence fast you have the opportunity to go within and be the observer. As you do this, it redirects your focus from doing to receiving. Receive what is given and brought to you without rejection or judgement. Patience and humility can be experienced from this. Additionally, focus on how you respond to events around you. Pay attention to the subtle energy shifts which occur. Practice embodying and becoming a spirit of total receptivity and silence. As you do this, understand this is the feminine receptive nature of your soul.

The silence fast usually has it best results when done at least one to three days. However, many have done it for up to 21 days. Determine the number of days you will do the silence fast, or be unctioned into it by Spirit. Many have gone on a silence fast and still communicate by writing. It is best to avoid this. Writing is another form of talking. Obviously silence fasts are best done when you do not have to go to work. As always, during a silence fast, or any kind of fast, increase prayer and meditation.

The positive talk fast is the next fast to consider. This gives you a very profound 'fast' movement toward Spirit. In a positive fast you only talk positive. You can only say constructive, optimistic, and cheerful things. You can not engage in negative, pessimistic, skeptical or discouraging words. You are only to talk about someone or something if it is complementary, encouraging and uplifting. Phrases or concepts that convey the message of can not, will not, or try, must be totally eliminated.

This exercise truly requires you to be honest with yourself. Many will carry on conversations about their shortcomings and will attest this is not a negative conversation. They say they are being realistic. Being realistic is a point of reference. During this exercise, lose your human reference point, and adopt the reference point of Spirit, where all things are possible.

Examine your feelings when you speak optimistically. Does it feel good, or does it create fear? Does it seem like a lie? Does it seem like a greater truth that had been hidden from you? By sincerely doing this, you get a glimpse of your every-day thought process that you normally do not see.

To do this fast, you must be diligently monitoring your every word. Think before you speak. For some who talk a lot, it may be necessary to talk less in order to choose your words carefully.

Another version of the positive fast is to monitor negative talk. It is often better to monitor negative talk prior to the positive talk fast. This prepares you to successfully engage in the positive fast. This exercise is done by monitoring how often you say something negative. Always keep a pen and small pad with you. Each time you make a negative statement, put a mark in the pad. After three days, count up how many marks you have generated.

Monitoring negative talk and the positive talk fasts are exercises that align your conscious dialog with that of Spirit. In the ultimate reality of Spirit abundance is natural. No lack, limitation or negativity exists. The goal of these fasts is not to deny your current state of being and thinking, but to fast toward another reference point. As these fasts are sincerely done, along with increased prayer and meditation, a subtle shift in the spirit of your mind and awareness can occur. A shift toward the abundant reality of Spirit.

Fasting to a positive reality by not watching news on television, is the last fast toward Spirit that will be discussed. In the name of investigative reporting, television news broadcasts sensationalism, fear and calamity. This is because news is a business, and fear based sensationalism sells best. This type of news is potentially damaging because it propagates a world vision of cruelty, callousness and violence. This desensitizes the heart and overwhelms the consciousness, thereby making it OK for the mind to accept a world of chaos.

Many on a spiritual path have given up this daily habit all together. Why assault your consciousness with programs designed for ratings instead of truth and social harmony. If you are addicted to news, or you feel you must know what is going on in the world, then fasting to Spirit by abstaining from news is the fast for you. These fasts can last a week, month or six months. If perchance Spirit within unctions you to permanently fast from TV news, you will be surprised how you won't miss a thing.

Let it be said that fasting from TV news in not a statement that spiritual people should be ostriches. Often, in order to realistically solve a problem, i.e., global disharmony, one must periodically remove themselves from the dilemma. After all, a pig does not know a pig stinks.

Fast toward Spirit within as often as possible. Let Spirit lead you, for the pace within will be quickened.

Thank you kind Spirit.

Common Sense Exercise: Midnight TV

If you wake up in the middle of the night, or have some spare time, get out of the habit of turning the TV on. Try meditation instead.

Thank you kind Spirit.

Energy Vampires, are they real?

John mumbled on continuously complaining about everything. He spoke in such a low monotonous voice that Judy had a hard time hearing him. So she listened intensely. Then, as she struggled with all of her might to follow his conversation, a feeling of frustration overcame her entire body. She realized he was aimlessly rambling from one topic to the next. When they got to their destination, Judy rapidly got out of the car. She had developed a splitting headache, between her eyes. Her energy was drained. She felt as limp as a dirty, wet dish rag. Then Judy realized, John was an energy vampire, and he sucked the life force right out of her.

Energy vampires are people who pull your vital life force in a way that leaves you weak, drained, and out of balance. A vampire is a person who often is self-absorbed, constantly needs help, continuously complains or talks a lot. When a vampire leaves someone drained, it is more than their annoying characteristics at play. The vampire is actually pulling the victim's energy. There is a real transmission of life force from the victim to the vampire. This transmission of energy can actually be seen or felt by spiritually developed individuals.

Most energy vampires are not consciously aware of the fact that they are draining life force from others. They usually learned how to drain energy when they were young. It is how they cope with life, and survive its stresses.

When you encounter an energy vampire, you have several choices. If you discern that the vampire is not stealing energy maliciously or consciously, then be kind. We all have been vampires one time or another when we have felt vulnerable or we needed help. If you have energy to spare, let them drink a little. If you feel your energy getting low, then pull upon the universal supply of unlimited energy. This can be done by prayer, or the simple intention to do so. Many people use the technique of visualizing white light coming down into the crown of their heads.

If you are in the midst of being drained of life-giving energy, and the above techniques are not working, then simply dismiss yourself from the physical proximity of the person. If you cannot physically get away, like riding in a car with a vampire, you can simply say a prayer of protection. Allow Spirit to put a shield of protective light around you. Within this impermeable shield you can keep your peace and harmony.

Needless to say, if you have a friend or relative who is a chronic vampire, you may wish to pull away from regular contact with this person. The drain of your energy over time is not healthy. However, if you do not wish to pull away from this person, but rather desire to help this person stop being a vampire. There may be something you can do. First, be aware that this may be a long and trying venture. Vampirism is a life-long pattern of survival. If the person has no desire to change, you cannot make them, and should not try. To help a chronic vampire, you might first send them spiritual love and light. Do not pray, visualize or ask the spiritual powers to directly stop this person from being a vampire. This may be interfering with this person's free will, or this person's desired creation or destiny. Just send love and light, and let Spirit determine what to do. Next, you pray for guidance, ask Spirit to show you how to proceed. Then be patient, and wait for guidance, even if it takes years to come. Guidance may come as a sign or message. You never know, Spirit may just bring the two of you together in conversation, and the person may directly ask for help, because they recognize that they turn people off.

If you discover you are an energy vampire, then know that the ultimate supply of energy is the Creator. Desire to receive all you need from Spirit, and not from man. Be silent, and practice pulling energy from the source within, instead of talking and looking for comfort without. Increase your prayer and meditation life. As you pray and meditate exceedingly night and day, your spiritual vibration will increase, and your need to receive energy from other people will automatically decrease. This sounds simple. But if you sincerely follow these simple instructions, you will find they work.

There is another important point to understand about energy exchange. Every time energy is taken does not mean a person is an energy vampire. I was at a Holy Ghost filled, talking-in-tongues, dancing-in-the-isles Christian church service. People were falling left and right on the floor in trance states as the Holy Ghost fell upon them. I was bathing in the spiritual energy. It was so high I could see a white cloud of Spirit in the air. It gave me a sensation of euphoria. I was drunk in Spirit. My entire body swelled and pulsated with light and healing energy.

I went to this service with a friend, Vonnella, with whom I had been meditating for years. We were very much in tune with each other's energy patterns. Then an amazing thing happened. Vonnella's spiritual eye opened. She could clearly see the flow of energy from one person to the next. She had never been able to see energy so clearly like this before. Then what she saw shocked and disturbed her. I was giving the praise leader, who had used her energy to usher in the Spirit at this service, a long engaging hug. Vonnella saw vast quantities of energy flowing from me into this person. She became concerned for my welfare. She felt that this person may drain me of so much energy it would take me weeks for recover. Vonnella quickly walked up behind me, stretched out her hand, and began to send me energy.

After the service, Vonnella told me what had happened. I laughed, and explained it was not my energy she was taking. I was a conduit for the Most High. The supply of energy I had was limitless. It was simply flowing through me.

181

In this situation, the praise leader was not a vampire. She was simply receiving a gift from the universal Spirit of love, and I was the vehicle to bring her that blessing. In fact, I was being blessed because the Spirit was flowing through me in the exchange.

The art of spiritual healing, works much the same as above. Healing energy flows from the healer to the one being healed. If the recipient of the healing is experienced in pulling energy, or truly desires the healing and has faith, then the person being healed will literally suck the healing energy from the healer. Pulling of healing energy is not vampirism. One of the best known stories explaining this healing phenomenon is the lady in the Bible who had an issue of blood. She knew that if she could just touch Jesus she would be healed. Unbeknown to Jesus, the lady touched his garment. Jesus asked, who touched him, because he felt virtue flow from him.

If you are to receive energy of any kind, it is a wonderful attribute to know how to pull this energy. All you really need is a desire and faith, like the lady with an issue of blood. Things that are desired are pulled to you by the great cosmic magnet called faith.

So have faith that you can open up and receive Light if you encounter an energy vampire. As you do this, you can no longer look upon anyone as a vampire. You will begin to see them as a blessing sent to you. You have been given another sacred opportunity to open up and let Universal Light and love flow through you.

Thank you kind Sprit.

Crystals, Gems and Healing.

Crystals, like herbs, plants, and the extracted medicines thereof, are God-given gifts for healing. Crystals, gems, rocks and minerals have been used extensively throughout the ages by many different cultures for their healing properties of body, mind and spirit. Crystals are the most effective in radiating healing energy. Even though there are many different beliefs on how crystals work, their molecular nature makes understanding their function quite simple. One mechanism of action will be proposed herein.

Crystals are highly organized molecular structures. If you shine a source light through the appropriately cut and polished crystal, the source light will be emitted as a laser. Thus a laser is simply a light - or energy - that has been focused to a given wavelength by a crystal. This specific uniform wavelength has different properties than the original source beam of light. As is so well known, this focused energy can be so intense it can cut physical matter.

Crystals used in healing work in much the same manner as crystals used to make lasers. To understand the healing property of crystals, one must first understand that the source energy that goes into healing crystals comes from humans. The human body emits energy beyond it borders. This is a well-documented biological fact. Dr. Leonard Ravitz at William and Mary University, calls it the human energy field, and says it fluctuates with mental and psychological stability. Dr. Robert Becker of Upstate Medical School refers to it as the direct current control system, which changes shape and strength with physiological and psychological changes. The ancients could see it, and called it the halo, or simply the light. The common modern term for it is the aura.

Human auras are a source of energy or light for the healing crystal. The crystal then takes the source energy from the person's energy field, and focuses it into another frequency. This new frequency radiates around the person and causes a shift in the person's energy field. This shift in the person's energy field causes a physical or mental change.

Spiritual healers that work with energy fields clearly understand that if you change a person's energy field, you also change their physical condition. Crystals simply change a person's energy field or aura. By doing so appropriately, healing may result.

There are hundreds of crystals. Each crystal has a different molecular composition and structure. Different crystals are therefore used to shift energy differently, and heal different problems. Just as different crystals are used to make different kinds of lasers.

The large volume of information on crystals prevents this guide book from going into further details on specific crystals. However, there are many source books on crystals.

Crystals, gems, rocks and minerals are truly God-given gifts for healing. However, if you do not have a natural attraction to crystals, or if Spirit is not directing you to crystals, it is not advisable to go out and invest hundreds of dollars buying crystals. This is a detailed healing art that can take years to learn. If Spirit does not lead you to crystals, you could waste precious time. Always remember the real power of healing is Spirit within. Crystals just help fine tune what Spirit has already given. So go within and let your light shine.

Thank you kind Spirit.

Chapter 7

Navigating the Matrix of Synchronicity

How to manifest without effort.

Synchronicity is a series of seemingly unrelated events or people that come together to create a larger outcome. Everything is perfectly organized and works out flawlessly without effort on your part. Synchronicity is life's experiences flowing in the harmony of oneness. Synchronicity is reaping where you have not sown.

Navigating the matrix of synchronicity is the art of perfectly receiving the abundance of the universe without getting in the way. The biggest allies that seal you fast to the tracks of this matrix is trust and faith. The biggest enemy that derails you from this matrix is an ego based, rational, masculine oriented mind.

If you do not look for the synchronicity of Spirit, you may disregard synchronized events and call them coincidences. By doing so, you may not follow the first step in a wonderfully orchestrated scenario of individual steps. By failing to complete the series of synchronized events, you may miss your blessing or manifestation.

Synchronicities can be simple, i.e., you need an item, and a friend unexpectedly delivers that item to you. Synchronicities can also be so complex that it involves hundreds of people around the world moving at once to create a spectacular, unexpected result.

Spirit communicates like a director, directing a massive symphony called life. There is no one way Spirit will lead you to synchronicity. Synchronicity is perfect communication and manifestation in operation. It may happen with and without any knowledge on your part.

The best way to clearly understand synchronicity is to look at an example. A beautiful and intricately detailed adventure I had last year will be shared to show how Spirit can direct your walk in the synchronized matrix of everyday life. As you read this story, pay attention to the many subtle synchronized events.

A friend that channels Spirit one day said to me. "I have been instructed to ask you to do a past life regression of me, and ask for Star Lady." After I got confirmation from Spirit, I did. A flowing celestial feminine being of light came forth and taught us many things. She told me I was a star child, and that my mission on earth involved helping to heal and balance the spiritual earth's energy. She also said that seven people would come together, then a journey would begin and much work would be done.

Simultaneous with this, my wife planned a weekend of meditation and ritual at a friend's house. My wife did not know of Star Lady's predictions of seven people coming together. Many more were invited, but seven showed up.

One of the weekend participants was a woman named Audri. She came from over eight hundred miles away with a prophetic message. "When the black, white and red hawks gather, the journey will begin." Amazingly, all three of these hawks flew by or landed in the back yard of this house that weekend, a house in the middle of a metropolitan area.

Audri had also been receiving information from the Council of Light about star people and star systems, as well as a matrix of sacred energy portals that were opening up around the world. She reported that one energy portal was located at the Tropic of Cancer at 23½ longitude. But she did not know the latitude. She needed this latitude to help complete her grid.

After this extraordinary weekend, I received a telephone call from a lady in Florida to arrange a speaking engagement for one of the teachers at the Institute. During the conversation, she declared out of the blue, "I am going to Mexico." Then before I knew it, I said "when we go to Mexico." I stopped myself in mid-sentence and asked, "why did I say that?" "Is Spirit telling me something?"

The next day I was on the telephone with a professional psychic Buddhist friend. I told her of the Mexico incidence. As we were talking, I looked out the window, and fifteen feet away was a white hawk staring at me. I have never seen a hawk in my 50 -foot-long back yard in Atlanta. This sign excited both of us; she said it was a good omen for the journey at hand, and she began prophesying to me. She saw me going to Mexico, and she saw me shooting up into the stars and exploding in massive star light. She did not know that Star Lady had called me star light.

That same day I had a meeting with the lady that channeled Star Lady. When I saw her she had on a necklace with a large silver hawk. I immediately stopped and ask. "Why did you wear that hawk today?" She responded. "I don't know. It doesn't go with what I have on. Spirit told me to wear it. So I put it on." I then shared with her why she wore it. The hawk was another sign for me to go to Mexico.

A few days later, as I awoke I had a vision. Spirit told me what day I should go to Mexico, and showed me a computer screen with the latitude and longitude of where I was to go. As I attempted to write the vision down, I forgot the geographical coordinates. Then Spirit immediately gave me another flash vision telling me to go to the library and look up the latitude and longitude of the city in Mexico that the lady from Florida was going to. At this time, I had no idea why Spirit was telling me to go to Mexico. But I decided I was definitely going.

I did not go to the library that day. The next morning I received a telephone call. It was Audri, who was still mapping the location of the energy portals. She emphatically told me that Spirit said I had something for her. She was looking for map coordinates. I shared my vision with her, and that I was to go to the library and look up the coordinates of this city in Mexico.

I hung up the telephone and went to the library. When I opened up the atlas, and saw that this small town in Mexico was at the 23½ longitude on the Tropic of Cancer, my excitement was so great, I literally screamed out in the library. This was the same longitude that Audri had been looking at to find a portal. The latitude was around 100. When I called Audri back with the coordinates, she was ecstatic. This latitude fit exactly in the grid of energy portals that Spirit had been giving her. (This portal information is now published in a book call the Diary of NOWTIME Prophecies by Audri Scott Williams.)

So now I knew why I was to go to Mexico. There was an energy portal there. Getting there was another dilemma. I had no money. My wife had stopped working several months before, and my source of income had dried up. Spirit was miraculously providing for our bills each month, but nothing was left.

Then an old friend called from Texas. He asked me if I could give a seminar there within the next several months. I told him I was going to Mexico in a few weeks, and asked would he market the seminar for me right now. His first response was no, that is not enough time. But after thinking, he realized he had the perfect opportunity to market it effectively. He went on to explain he was producing two large multi-cultural concerts at that time. I could speak at them for exposure, and we could book a speaking engagement the next day. So kind Spirit had provided funds for me to go to Mexico by stopping through Texas.

One month after receiving the message to go to Mexico all plans had been made. I was on my journey, and what a journey it was!

Getting to Real De Catorce, the destination in Mexico, was a pilgrimage. This small city was nestled in the Eastern Sierra Madre mountains, with a one-lane cobblestone road carved through a mountain side as the only access. The city had a population of 2,000. The entire population shared one telephone and fax located at a store front. The lady in Florida had a spiritual Native American friend that lived there. She faxed her the information that several people from Atlanta were coming, and asked her to please make hotel reservations for us.

The actual trip took two days, by airplane, bus and car. While driving, the signs from Spirit continued to flow. We saw dozens upon dozens of peregrines - a falcon and close cousin to the hawk - lining the road side, almost like a welcoming party showing us the way.

While on a commercial bus, I saw a Mexican tour guide book, and to my surprise, Real De Catorce was in it. A great miracle involving St. Francis of Assisi's statue had occurred there. The statue was reported to have moved on its own from one cathedral to another small church. As a result thousands of catholics from all over Mexico and around the world pilgrimage to this little town every September and October for healings. I then realized this sacred spot was known to others.

When I got to Real De Catorce, the Native American lady that had made our reservations introduced herself and said. "I saw your name written on the fax. But I cannot remember that name. When I think of you, I see stars exploding in great light. So I have renamed you. Your name is Star Light."

Now that we were in this small town in Mexico, we realized the journey had just begun. The Native American had been receiving information from Spirit about the specific location of an energy portal that was about to reopen. A portal that had something to do with the stars. There had been no communication with this lady and Audri. But the information they separately received was remarkably similar.

The Native American told us the exact location of the portal was on top of a mountain call El Quemado. El Quemado has been the sacred ground for the indigenous Huichole Indians for hundreds of years. It is the location for their sacred peyote fires. She received permission from the indigenous Mexican Indians for us to go there and stay over night. We were to go there upon its spiritual reopening, a momentous occasion.

The top of this mountain was nine thousand feet high. We went part of the way on horse back, with mules carrying the camping supplies. When it got too steep for the horses, we had to walk.

So there I was. On a mountain top in Mexico, a sacred energy portal just reopening; a place where the locals see so many UFO's, they consider it a normal thing. There were twelve of us there, a perfect number of completion - six men and six women. This was also a perfect balance of masculine and feminine energy. We did not know each other. We did not even speak the same language. Several small groups making up the twelve had come from different parts of the world. We each had our own individual stories of how Spirit had led us there.

We moved into ceremony and ritual as a magnificently beautiful sun began to set over the valley below. Ritual, drumming, flute playing, dancing and song echoed into the crisp night air. We all knew a way was being created for the flow of energy. A cleansing was occurring. Mother Earth was rejoicing.

As the night grew late, the others nestled down into their sleeping bags to stay warm, and go to sleep. But I was too charged with energy. I stayed up throughout the night, praying, meditating, dancing, and giving thanks. Then it happened. Without warning, I shot up out of my body, straight into the midnight sky. In a great flash, I exploded into star light. Then as soon as it had happened, my center of vision was back in my body.

The experience hit me so suddenly, I was startled in amazement. After regrouping and reflecting on the moment. I shouted out to the heavens in thanks giving. Thank you kind Spirit! Thank you for this journey into the light!

I knew somehow I had grown closer to Spirit, and my home in the stars. This concluded the first synchronized cycle of my visiting energy portals.

Since that time, I have miraculous and synchronisticly traveled to two more energy portals described by Audri. Upon arriving at the general location of the portals, a local person synchronisticly directed me to the exact center of the portal. Then another amazing synchronicity appeared. All three energy portals had their center on a double pointed mountain, with water near by.

My adventure of stars, hawks, mountain tops and energy portals is just a small example of how Spirit uses seemingly isolated events and people to create a wonderfully synchronized experience.

Synchronicity is an awesome form of multidimensional communication and manifestation. Spirit is not linear. Spirit's language is multifaceted. It expresses itself simultaneously in multiple directions for the good of all concerned. Spirit is a matrix of nonlinear love and creation. By experiencing synchronicity in your life, you begin to get a glimpse of the marvelously woven tapestry that life truly is. By experiencing synchronicity, Spirit is communicating to you its real nature. Spirit is calling you home. For you are also a being of nonlinear creation.

There is an art to flowing in synchronicity. Trust the process. Be positive and optimistic. Lose all attitudes of lack and scarcity. Believe all things are possible. To flow in synchronicity, never think that anything is a coincidence. Look at every event as being perfectly synchronized. Quietly expect your life to be lived in synchronicity every second of the day. Even if it is not apparent to you, know and trust that it is in divine order. Living a life in unattached expectation opens up all kinds of opportunities for abundance to come in. In fact, your very attitude of expectation draws abundance to you. However, there is a fine line between unattached expectation, and open lust.

Do not lust after abundance or anything. The act of lust drives it away. To expect in lust means that you are emotionally tied to the outcome. Being emotionally tied to an outcome will cause you to error in your movements. You may see a potential way to receive a thing, move prematurely out of your own will toward it, and miss the real synchronized flow. Also being emotionally tied to an outcome often invites worry.

Worry is spiritual shortsightedness. Worry is a statement of your true underlying belief that it possibly will not manifest. It is possible you might not receive the thing desired. All kinds of possibilities arise in worry. This underlying belief is your prayer to the universe, and the universe answers you by saying: "because there are so many possibilities, let's through a dice and see which one hits." In other words, you have not sent a clear message to the universe. By doing so, you have chosen to play the role of a victim.

A victim is bound by circumstances, and lustfulness is being bound by desire. Spirit is free! Whenever you are bound, you cannot move freely. The very act of synchronicity means to move freely in the ebb and flow of Spirit's will.

This free movement is the hallmark of the true spiritual master. A true master is exceedingly abundant in the physical, despite the fact a master has given up all desires and wants in the physical. The spiritual master does nothing for prosperity's sake. It just comes to them through synchronicity. Masters reap where they have not sown.

Living in perfect synchronicity means you do not struggle to make things happen. You simply be, and everything comes together.

Living in perfect synchronicity is living a life in which your every step is in sync with your greatest good, and as you move step by step toward your Highest Nature creating abundance, love and prosperity on all levels, your walk is beautifully guided. All you have to do is listen and obey.

Obedience to Spirit is another important concept to incorporate into your life in order to flow in synchronicity. Obedience is often the vehicle which moves you from one synchronized event, to the next. For example, I had no idea when Star Lady told me I was a star child, a series of synchronized events would have me standing on a mountain top in Mexico shooting up into the stars. If obedience had not been an integral part of the entire process, it could have never happened. I had to be obedient to do the initial past life regression. I had to be obedient and follow up on my Spirit-led impulsive telephone conversation about going to Mexico. The lady with the hawk necklace was obedient and wore the necklace, thus giving me a sign. Audri was obedient and called about the map coordinates. I had to be obedient and look them up.

One must even be obedient in thought. When the visionary message to leave for Mexico on a Sunday came, I had to be obedient in thought and believe I would go on a Sunday. Even though I could not afford to go, and the credit cards were almost maxed out, I believed I would go. I lovingly told my wife that I was going to Mexico. Because of my obedience in consciousness, I was quietly waiting - in absolute expectation - to find a way to get to Mexico. When my friend from Texas called, I recognized the opportunity. If I had not been obedient in consciousness, and did not have the faith I was going to Mexico, I would have never thought to ask about scheduling a presentation with such short notice. Lack of faith stops the flow of Spirit, and makes obedience difficult to impossible.

When discussing obedience, an important distinction must be made between obedience to the word of Spirit that is written in your heart, and obedience to the rigid dogma of organized religions. To perfectly ride the matrix of synchronicity, one must be obedient to every unction, knowing and essence of Spirit within and without. One cannot effectively navigate this matrix if one blindly follows the rigid rules of religion. These rules have often been created by man, and disguised as God's will.

The role of religion is perfectly summarized by Vivekananda. "It is good to be born in a church, but it is bad to die there. It is good to be born a child, but bad to remain a child. Churches, ceremonies, symbols are good for children; but when the child is grown up, he must burst, either the church or himself... The end of all religion is the realization of God..."

Religion is supposed to 're' form a 'legion' with Spirit. To re-form a legion with Spirit one must: first, choose in each and every moment to create a higher expression of Spirit within; second, be obedient to the flow of Spirit after this choice has been make; and finally, take it one step at a time.

One step at a time is how you navigate the matrix of synchronicity. For years I have talked to people who pondered why Spirit only gives them instructions as to what to do next? Why will Spirit not give us more? Then our reasoning went on like this. Well if Spirit would tell me more, I would be obedient and follow the instructions perfectly. So I don't understand, why won't Spirit tell me more?

I received a wonderful revelation from Spirit while I was writing this book. I was getting anxious about finishing the book. It had already taken me longer than expected. Even though I knew not to have expectations, and that I was to flow with the process, a feeling of urgency was befalling me. Spirit instructed me to finish by a certain time, which was quickly approaching. In my predicament, I started writing and asking Spirit a flurry of questions. Who should I send the book to for preview? What about publishers picking it up? How much money will I make? After each question I got either a curious pause, or a written response that gave little new information. Then an interesting dialog started.

Spirit said: "That is all. Focus on finishing the book first. Then ask these questions. As far as I am concerned, dismiss the above questions from your mind, and the answers. Focus on one thing at a time. The thing that is in front of you. You know how it works. One step at a time."

I responded: "OK." Then Spirit went on: "Understand this. The future holds many great possibilities. Even now we are working on great things in your future. Better opportunities than was listed above, or even imagined may open up. If you are focused on just the above (questions), you shoot down these opportunities."

Spirit went on to write through me: "Now here is a lesson. Many wonder why Spirit tells you one step at a time. It is for the reason stated above. Your future holds so much that the only truth is the one right now. I can speculate what will happen way out in the future, and indeed I do at times, and so does your psychics (a lot more in error than they should), but if I did this, I would be limiting your future, or even predestinating it. You must make a decision right now, and the rest will fall into place. This is the secret of walking the matrix of synchronicity.

Also another point is when I do predict a series of events way out into the future, it is because you have created such a track of destiny in your life that your future is almost unavoidable. The classic example of you creating such a background of movement that your future is unavoidable can be seen in the physical death of the body.

Each and every human has the God given ability to ascend. That is to dematerialize your physical body and never experience physical death. Many of your great masters of the past have done this, and the best of these masters can rematerialize their body at will.

However, one must start to evolve spiritually early enough to be able to accomplish this beautiful feat. If a person is sixty and then decides to start to grow spiritually, there may not be enough time for them to evolve enough to ascend. It can be predicted with assurance that this person will lose their physical body at the end of this incarnation. The person's entire life pattern has tracked that person to this fate. But know this. This is not a bad result. The mission was accomplished. They learned, experienced, created, had fun, felt sadness. This experience has edified their soul, and pleased me. They will have another chance to try again, and again, and again."

I can not explain how great this revelation was for me. We are given instructions one step at a time to keep us living in the present moment. Right now is how to navigate the matrix. A ship in a storm is concerned with navigating the present wave, not the wave that may come an hour from now.

Also, information is given one step at a time, for if it were not, we would limit our creative potential by predestining our future with plans and goals. The next best and greatest thing to create is what lies before us. Because what may lie before us, may be greater than our minds could have ever imagined.

Now, let it be known and clear, we can choose to get answers about our daily life path way out into the future. If you choose to do this consistently, you will definitely get answers. But these answers may not come from your Highest Nature, or be for your greatest good. Also by demanding answers, you no longer ride the fluid matrix of synchronicity; you create your own rigid, inflexible path. You are ordering the universe around. You can choose to do this. Many have, and do it well. But consider this: if you choose this path, you are operating out of the mind of a man, which automatically imposes severe limitations.

A delicate balance must be found. It is to your advantage to form in your mind the greatest, highest vision of your future in

Spirit. Then, you must know that you are what Spirit says you are. By doing so, you start to track yourself into spiritual evolution. However, you must be constantly open to allow Spirit to increase and change this vision as you awaken into what Spirit is. The best time to be open to expand this vision is right now.

Timing is critical when riding the matrix of synchronicity. This statement is almost obvious. You must be in the right place, at the right time, for synchronicity to work. If not, a series of perfectly orchestrated events come to a halt.

The concept of timing is so important that it must be looked at in detail. First, recall that time is a dimension which exists in physical reality. In the universe of massive expansion, thought forms travel at immense speeds, thus warping the time line and creating a space-time continuum.

In the space-time continuum the universe can fold upon itself making two distant points in space move closer together. Therefore, in the continuum any two points in space can be brought together by simply folding the fibers of the matrix. Additionally, any two points in time can come together by folding the matrix. Thus the space-time continuum makes the matrix of synchronicity a series of events that are not happening in different locations at different times. All of the events are happening right now, in the present moment, at the same place. Consequently, the entire Mexico adventure that I described, did not occur over a couple of months, but it happened in one split moment in space-time. It was as if I were in a black hole, and right there with me was everyone and everything that was needed for this extraordinary event. The people and events were attracted to me in this black hole because a black hole has such great gravitational pull, it draws everything in the immediate universe closer to it.

A black hole is a real physical occurrence in space. It is a very small region of space-time with a gravitational field so intense that nothing can escape, not even light. This extremely dense structure

197

sucks in everything in the universe that is close to it, including stars. Thus the analogy of a black hole is used here. Each point on the spiritual matrix is as a black hole attracting to it all that is needed.

Your ability to focus in Spirit in the moment creates a gravitational pull. The greater your ability to be in Spirit in the present moment, the greater your spiritual gravitational pull will attract everything needed. In other words, your present moment is a black hole that attracts to it by folding space-time and bringing to it simultaneously the events and people needed to create.

This is why right now is the only time we have. For right now the entire universe has unfolded and refolded to create our entire life, as well as individual events. If we begin to think thus, we likewise begin to overcome the illusion of lack. For everything we need is right here. Simply fold the matrix of space and time with the power of your thoughts, and there it is.

Loving, prosperous thoughts fold the matrix easily. Thoughts of fear, unfold the matrix like a strong whirl wind. These e-motions (energy in motions) are uncontrolled and erratic. They violently tear the matrix, leaving you stranded in no-man's land.

As discussed earlier in this book, thoughts of fear give rise to anger, hatred, depression and jealousy. These e-motions likewise unravel the universe (uni =one verse) surrounding the black hole, and disrupt synchronized events.

Let us further explain the concept of a black hole by examining what ancient scriptures said about creation. Many ancient teachings state that the Creator God created all heaven and earth from a nothingness, a void, a blackness. This was the ancients' way of describing what we describe as the black hole. From this nothingness, all was created in seven phases as the Egyptians say, or seven days in the Bible.

This brings in the next concept. In the creation story, there are seven stages in which heaven and earth were created. There were seven black dots from which all the known and unknown universe was created. These dots are connected in tandem creating a line. Thus, one line in the Creator's great cosmic matrix of synchronicity now existed. As the Creator breathed life into other intelligent creator beings - like humans - the lines and fabric of the universe continued to expand from the creative centers of untold numbers of black dots, each black dot being the center of each creator being in that moment.

We are made in the image and likeness of God, and we also create from a void or black hole in this same fashion. Hence, a grand fabric of reality has been or is being created.

Now, let's imagine an impossible situation to make a point. Let's say the Creator got upset on day three of creation, and in anger disrupted everything in creation on that day. For the intricately detailed universe to function, day three would have to be dismantled and re-created. This example, fortunately, could not happen. The Creator is harmony and love. However, the concept conveyed is simple.

If you lose your composure right now and get upset, you disrupt the synchronized events that are happening simultaneously in the eternal present moment. You must now start anew, and create the entire series of events again. The more upset you become, the more off-center you are taken, and the greater the synchronized events have been thrown off. As a result, you experience disharmony or stress in your life. If you use stress as an indicator that you have unraveled the matrix, getting back on track is easy.

We are creating our reality in every moment, in every second, of every day. If our thoughts have origin in Spirit, the possibilities are limitless. We can literally create unspeakable joy, unimaginable peace and untold abundance in a moment, in a twinkling of an eye. We simply must surrender our will to the divine order of Spirit, have faith, and be open to receive and become unconditional love.

In each moment of time that we create, and move on to the next moment, and ride the wave of synchronicity, we are creating and recreating the matrix. As we continue to move in the great cosmic ocean of love, we are attracted to the center of the matrix. In that center, oneness exists. All lines in the cosmic matrix lead to that center, the original great void or great black hole. As we reach the core, we have returned home. The I am, that I Am, is realized. The One and only true God, the Most High Spirit, the Source of Sources, the All In All is present in her\his full creative potential. In this black hole of pure potentiality there is light, love and truth.

Our journey home, is a journey of creating one infinite moment in space-time, right after another infinite moment in space-time. Finding our way back home is easy if we listen to the great call of the One. It sends fragrances of love, peace and harmony into the universe. As we still ourselves, we pick up the heavenly aromas, and know the direction. But if we are rushed and pressed, we will never take time to smell the flowers, and we will miss the secret of life.

Flow naturally and peacefully in each and every moment. For in this moment you are deciding great things. In this moment months, years, and even lifetimes are simultaneously occurring synchronisticly. Will you receive it in the peaceful meditative state of being, or will you destroy it by doing and thinking with the mind of a man? It is your choice. You have free will. What will you choose this very moment?

If you choose fear, and its related emotions, you stay separated, constantly in a fiery wind storm, destroying all that has been created. You therefore exist in a literal hell created by yourself. If you choose thoughts of love, compassion, gratitude, harmony, peace, and oneness, you stay centered in Spirit, in the moment. Then you can smell the fragrance of the One, and return home.

In summary let's review how you must see the matrix to navigate it successfully. You are in a black dot, and within the dot you have everything you need in the present moment. Do not think you can successfully look to your past experiences to help you make a decision now. This is because your past experience was in another moment in time, or another black hole. Look only to the present moment, and then be guided as to what you are receiving from Spirit within. As you make a pure, unadulterated decision in that moment for your highest good, for the union with the All In All, you then recreate yourself all over again in another infinitely beautiful and higher black hole. Repeat the process and you move again, and again, and again. Choose correctly at each universal opportunity of the now, and you begin to travel exponentially back home.

Once you move into the All In All, and become one with it all, you no longer navigate the matrix. You are the matrix. You are every creation, every decision, every event that has ever happened. Now it's time to start all over again. But this time a greater, grander universe will be yours.

Special note: I give homage to Spirit, through the Council of Light, who has given me the information and experiences in this chapter.

Thank you kind Spirit.

Afterword

The information in this book was inspired by the Most High Spirit. If you follow all of the guidelines within this guide, not just the ones that are comfortable for you, you will begin to awaken spiritually.

Spirituality comes by walking the path in every moment of life. When the going gets rough, remember these are the times when the learning can be greatest. I pray that this book will make your path to enlightenment easier and more rewarding.

The next step in your journey is always the most important one. Step with confidence, love and humility. As you continue to grow in Spirit, refer to this manual for inspiration and guidance. Take notes in your diary, and tell me of your experiences. Let me know how this book may be improved. And always remember to say "Thank You Kind Spirit."

Appendix

Seminars & Workshops

Seminars, workshops and classes are available for your spiritual groups, churches or organizations. Any topic covered in this book, including many others, are given by Dr. Muldrow. Workbooks are provided with selected workshops. Topics include, but are not limited to

Navigating the Matrix of Synchronicity. Information received from Spirit on how to manifest effortlessly is presented in seminar, class, or workshop format. More details are presented in these sessions than is presented in "The Common Sense Guide for Spirituality."

Woman Awaken: Man Die. Riveting, interactive workshops to further illuminate the truth about the death process for men, and the awakening for women. Scriptures and ancient teaching from Egypt are given to back up this workshop on spiritual balancing of masculine and feminine energy.

The Art of Meditation. Making prayer and meditation a way of life is the key to evolving spiritually. In these seminars, workshops or classes, spiritual insight is given on how to become the prayer and meditation; thus making it a way of life.

The Nature of Reality. The illusion of this world is a perceived trap that prevents our spiritual evolution. Information received from Spirit, is given in this workshop to turn the illusionary trap of physical reality, into a lure that captures spiritual freedom.

The Spiritual Journey. Details on the pitfalls and mountain-top experiences on the path to oneness are illuminated in this interactive workshop.

Other Seminars, Workshops & Classes. A wide variety of subjects ranging from visual affirmations, to spiritual stress management for the workplace and at home, are given by Dr. Lycurgus L. Muldrow.

For additional information call or write:

Institute for Divine Wisdom, Inc.
P.O. Box 491948
Atlanta, Ga 30349

Phone: 404 525-1212

Web site: divinewisdom.net

Retreats

The Institute for Divine Wisdom sponsors spiritual retreats to various locations including Real De Catorce, Mexico. If you are interested in obtaining information call, write or visit the Institute for Divine Wisdom web site.

Order Form

Telephone orders: Call toll free *888 281-5170.* Have your Visa, MasterCard, or American Express ready. Price includes freight and handling charges.

Mail Orders & Fax Orders: Call *888 281-5170* for instructions, mailing address and total cost including freight and handling charges.

Please send the following books.

_____No. of Books___

Your Name:_____

Address:_____

City:_____State:____Zip:_____

Check []:   Credit card: [] Visa, [] MasterCard, [] AMEX

Card number_____

Name on card_____Exp. date____

For additional information contact:
Institute for Divine Wisdom Publishing
P. O. Box 491948
Atlanta, GA 30349
(404) 525-1212